Дон Кихот
Don Quixote

MIKHAIL BULGAKOV

Дон Кихот
Don Quixote

Edited by
Margarita Marinova
and Scott Pollard

The Modern Language Association of America
New York 2014

85 Broad Street, New York, New York 10004
www.mla.org

To order MLA publications, visit www.mla.org/books. For wholesale and international orders, see www.mla.org/bookstore-orders.

The MLA office is located on the island known as Mannahatta (Manhattan) in Lenapehoking, the homeland of the Lenape people. The MLA pays respect to the original stewards of this land and to the diverse and vibrant Native communities that continue to thrive in New York City.

Cover illustration: woodcut by Nikolai Piskarev for Anatoly Lunacharsky's Освобождённый Дон Кихот ("The Liberated Don Quixote"), 1922. General Research Division, the New York Public Library, Astor, Lenox and Tilden Foundations

Texts and Translations 29
ISSN 1079-252X

Library of Congress Cataloging-in-Publication Data

Bulgakov, Mikhail, 1891–1940, author.
[Don Kikhot.] Don Quixote / Mikhail Bulgakov ; edited by Margarita Marinova and Scott Pollard.
pages cm. — (Texts and translations, ISSN 1079-2538 ; 29)
Includes bibliographical references.
ISBN 978-1-60329-149-1 (pbk.) —
ISBN 978-1-60329-151-4 (EPUB) —
ISBN 978-1-60329-152-1 (Kindle)
1. Don Quixote (Fictitious character)—Drama. I. Marinova, Margarita, editor. II. Pollard, Scott, 1958– editor. III. Title.
PG3476.B78D66 2014 891.73'42—dc23 2014011358

Contents

ACKNOWLEDGMENTS

At Christopher Newport University, we would like to thank two deans, Douglas Gordon and Steven Breese; two provosts, Richard Summerville and Mark Padilla; and two English Department chairs, Tracey Schwarze and Jean Filetti, for their support of this project. We are grateful for the help of Professors Denise Gilman and Tanya Sweet of Theater CNU; Annie Foster-LeVasseur and Jennifer Bukovsky, the student directors who organized three readings of drafts of the play; and the actors who participated in those readings: Sarah Bella Alderson, Grace Beach, Chris Blake, Cate Carney, David Carter, Alex Cirves, Jeff Gallo, Luis Gonzalez, Billy Harley, Martin Lawrence, Jake Mills, Jamie Monahan, Johnny O'Malley, Katie Parker, Austin Pike, Charlie Retzlaff, Caroline Rigby, Levi Shrader, and Kyle Talley. This project was also generously funded by an NEH summer stipend (2011). Finally, we owe a huge debt of gratitude to Michael Henry Heim, whose input was fundamental to the shaping of the translation through to its final form.

INTRODUCTION

The Russian *Don Quixote*

In the summer of 1937, the artistic director of the Vakhtangov Theater, Vasily Vasilyeevich Kuza, asked Mikhail Afanasyevich Bulgakov if he would be willing to do a stage adaptation of Zola's *Nana*, Maupassant's *Bel-Ami*, or Balzac's *Eugénie Grandet*. No longer permitted to publish his original work, Bulgakov must have felt pressure to accept any commission whatever, yet he declined the offer because none of the proposed works appealed to him at the time. It was not until Kuza suggested *Don Quixote* that Bulgakov finally signed a contract with the Vakhtangov Theater, which committed him to producing a script within a year of 3 December.

He started working on the play immediately but then dropped the project in order to focus exclusively on revising Мастер и Маргарита, the novel that was to make his name known around the world on its publication years after his death. Although he did not return to Дон Кихот until June, he managed to produce a complete draft of the adaptation in less than a month, while the Bulgakovs were vacationing in a small town to the south of Moscow. In July, he was back in the capital revising the play and reading the novel in the original, his encounter with the text so inspiring that he even started using Spanish in letters to his wife.[1] By early September he had completed a version he felt fairly satisfied with. Later he would remove a few scenes because the play was a little too long. The final version, which was used for the translation in this volume, bears the date 18 December 1938.

Things ran less smoothly for the play after that. All works of literature had to be submitted to a rigorous censorship process. The play did not pass the initial review by Glavrepertkom (the Main Repertory Committee, the Soviet euphemism for the censors in charge of theatrical works) until November 1939, and it did not receive official approval until 17 January 1940. The delay was extended even further by the last-minute need to replace the director, who had fallen ill. As a result, the Vakhtangov Theater could not meet the production deadline of 1 January specified in the contract and lost its rights to premiere the work. Desperate to see at least one of his scripts performed on the stage, Bulgakov sent his Дон Кихот to several other theaters: the Pushkin Dramatic Theater in Leningrad, the Griboedov Theater in Tbilisi, and other, smaller theaters in the provinces. Thus, though commissioned by the Vakhtangov, the play premiered at the Pushkin Dramatic Theater. Unfortunately, by the time it went into production in the autumn of 1940, its author was dead.

Had he been alive, Bulgakov would most likely have been pleased with the warm reception that both critics and audiences gave the play, though it is anybody's guess whether he would have approved of the title character's interpretation by Nikolai Cherkasov, one of the theater's best male actors at the time, who was to become known in the West for his portrayal of Ivan the Terrible in Sergei Eisenstein's celebrated film.[2] His Don Quixote, as the critics noted, was always melancholy, "lyrical and intellectual" (Wright 240). The humor with which Bulgakov had infused his play was completely lost in Cherkasov's interpretation. The comic streak in Don Quixote's character was later resurrected in the great Ruben Simonov's performance when the play opened at the Vakhtangov Theater on 8 April 1941. The critics were less impressed by this interpretation of Cervantes's hero, however, and their displeasure with the character portrayal by the actor spilled over to the author of the play and the adaptation as a whole, which was found to be too realistic and thus too removed from Cervantes (241). The negative reviews were hardly surprising, given the long history of Russia's insistence on seeing the title character in a predominantly tragic light.

Russian critics and readers traditionally interpreted Don Quixote as a Romantic hero, the symbol of an idealistic dreamer ill suited to the realities of life. Russian writers from Nikolai Gogol and Ivan Turgenev to Dmitry Merezhkovsky and Fyodr Sologub identified closely with Don Quixote, turning him into the exemplar of the troubled artist. Bulgakov engaged both these traditions in his adaptation of the novel, and his interpretation of the character should be viewed in the broader context of Russian letters' history of obsession with its symbolic significance.[3]

Russian readers came to know Don Quixote and Sancho much later than their West European counterparts. It was not until 1769 that the novel was first translated (from the French) into Russian. Although of poor quality, the translation garnered enough attention from the native audience to secure a permanent place for the novel on the bookshelves of Russian literati. The subsequent thirty-four translations over the next two hundred years attest to the fact that Russian readers felt a particular affinity for the Knight of the Doleful Countenance and his squire.

The popularity of the novel in Russia can be further measured by the great number of children's versions (thirty-nine between the mid-nineteenth century and 1940), ballets (the classic Petipa version was the most often performed over the years), operas (noteworthy is Jules Massnet's version, originally starring the great Russian bass Chaliapine), operettas (the 1926 musical comedy by Alexandra Brushtein was especially popular), and cinematic adaptations (in particular the 1934 and the 1957 films).

Among the several translations of the novel available to him at the time, Bulgakov chose M. V. Watson's Остроумно-изобретательный идальго Дон-Кихот Ламанчский (1907).[4] Notes in the margins of the book, which is preserved in the writer's archives, as well as references to it in the play's manuscript suggest that it was his primary Russian text, though he may also have consulted the more recent translation by B. A. Krzhevski and A. A. Smirnov, printed in 1929 by Academia, a respected publisher. Although the professed goal of the Academia editors' series of new translations of the canon echoed Stalin's call to "take possession of this treasure, to rework its contents critically, to make it accessible to the builders of the socialist society, and to utilize it for the formation of the new man in a classless society" (Turkevich 191–92), the Krzhevski-Smirnov version, which went through many editions, is still considered among the most faithful translations because it succeeds in striking a balance between modern and archaic language and preserving Cervantes's linguistic plasticity and concreteness and richness of imagery.

Working from this new version as well as from a few older popular Russian versions of the novel, several Soviet writers had undertaken the task of producing dramatic adaptations of *Don Quixote* before Bulgakov. Most notable are the play by Anatoly Lunacharsky (the highly influential people's commissar of enlightenment) called Освобождённый Дон-Кихот (1922), which interpreted Don Quixote as a symbol of the Soviet intelligentsia, and Georgy Chulakov's Дон Кихот (1935), which focused on the opposition between the "abstract dreaminess of Don Quixote and the equally abstract rationalism of Carrasco" (Turkevich 196). That Bulgakov's version surpasses artistically both these works is evidenced by the play's consistent performance history in the years since its first production. Three factors contributed to its continuing relevance: first, Bulgakov's immense talent as a writer and playwright set him apart from other contemporary dramatists; second, Cervantes's text had special resonances for Bulgakov,[5] whose life, like Quixote's and Cervantes's, was nearing its end; finally, the experiences of Bulgakov in Soviet Russia enabled him to infuse the adaptation with the poignancy and conviction of a fellow sufferer, tragically familiar with social and political attempts to control the creative imagination.

Bulgakov's Life and Times

Mikhail Afanasyevich Bulgakov was born on 15 May 1891 in Kiev (now the capital of Ukraine, then part of the Russian Empire), the first of seven children, to Russian parents: Afanasy Ivanovich Bulgakov, an assistant professor at the Kiev Theological Academy, and Varvara Mikhailovna Bulgakova, a teacher. As both grandfathers of the author were priests, religion played an important role in his childhood and youth. Questions of the place of religious leaders in society and the church's promise of salvation were recurrent themes in his creative output throughout his life. Although Bulgakov struggled with theological explanations of the meaning of life and devoted much time to philosophical study as a young man, he chose to pursue a secular career, and on graduating from the First Kiev Gymnasium in 1904, he entered the medical school of Kiev University. His career choice was most likely influenced by his two uncles and stepfather, Ivan Voskresensky, who were medical doctors. In 1913, Bulgakov married his first wife, Tatyana Lappa. (He was to marry three times.) After he received his diploma in 1916, the couple moved to a small village in the Smolensk region, where he worked as a physician. He was later transferred to the district town of Vyazma to serve as head of the infectious and venereological department at the local hospital. His experiences as a country doctor are recorded in stories that were later collected and published as Записки юного врача (1925–27). By 1918 he had had enough of country life and returned to Kiev, which at the time—the end of the First World War and the beginning of the civil war that followed the October Revolution—was being fought over by Germans, Ukrainian nationalists, the Red Army (the Bolsheviks), and the White Army (the anti-Bolsheviks). His two brothers enlisted in the White Army and eventually emigrated to Paris. Bulgakov had a very different fate. He too joined the White Army but was sent to the Caucasus, where he fell ill with typhus and was thus unable to retreat with the army and follow his brothers into exile. He was never to see them again; his requests to be granted permission to travel abroad were repeatedly denied by the Soviet government.[6]

While still in the Caucasus, Bulgakov gave up medicine and turned to journalism. From then on he devoted himself to writing, trying his pen at various genres. In 1919, he published his first book, a collection of feuilletons called Грядущие перспективы, which afford a glimpse of the talent for keen social observation and piercing satire that were to become his trademark. In 1921, his small family moved to Moscow, the new capital of the Soviet state, and he dedicated his efforts to establishing a literary reputation for himself among the socialist intelligentsia. His first serious literary work, a novel called Белая гвардия, was a thinly veiled autobiographical account of the experiences of intellectuals and tsarist officers during the civil war in Ukraine. Though published in part in the journal Россия in 1925, its first full Russian edition appeared only in 1966. Three novellas followed Белая гвардия in quick succession: Роковые яйца (1924), Дьяволиада (1925), and Собачье сердце (1925). They were received favorably by critics and general audiences alike.

Heartened by his success with fiction, Bulgakov ventured into a genre for which he had always had a special fondness: drama. In 1926 he turned Белая гвардия into a play, Дни Турбиных. It premiered at the Moscow Art Theater, then run by the famous theater directors Konstantin Stanislavsky and Vladimir Nemirovich-Danchenko, and immediately established Bulgakov's reputation as the preeminent Soviet playwright. Reportedly Stalin, who in the years after Lenin's death in 1926 was emerging as his successor, greatly appreciated the play, which ensured its continued run despite criticism in the press that bemoaned the lack of a strong Communist hero.

The Communist Party's literary watchdogs had a point. During the 1920s, there were two types of serious drama in Russia: melodrama and plays about the revolution and the civil war. The latter type (to which Дни Турбиных belongs) may be subdivided into drama that dealt with these monumental events in a foreign context, like Sergei Tretiakov's Слышишь, Москва?! (1923) and Рычи, Китай! (1924), and plays that investigated their aftermath. Classic examples of the second type are Vsevolod Vishnevsky's Первая конная (1929) and Vladimir Bill-Belotserkovsky's Шторм (1924). Usually conceived as epics in dramatic form, such works revolved around a Communist hero of mythic proportions and carried a clear ideological message about the triumph of the Soviet state. Bulgakov's Дни Турбиных breaks with these genre expectations and subtly questions the use of theater as Communist propaganda.[7]

In the play, as in the novel from which it was adapted, Bulgakov's interests lie not with the victorious advent of the Red Army forces, which would have been the expected focus of a work about the period, but with the campaign to crush a German-supported Ukraine. Against this political backdrop, Дни Турбиных shows the profound changes that war and revolution have on family life. Bulgakov's compassionate treatment of the Turbins, a family sympathizing with the Whites, is unique when compared with the uniformly hostile interpretations of the White cause in the literature of the time. Much like Anton Chekhov's Вишнёвый сад, Дни Турбиных centers not so much on the clash between two orders or the ultimate victory of the new over the old as on the unavoidable passing of a refined and basically idealistic way of life. Clearly Bulgakov's sympathetic treatment of a White family could not be overlooked for long: in 1928, the play was removed from the stage with an official ban that lasted for four years, until his personal appeal lifted it.

The sequel to Дни Турбиных, Бег, which Bulgakov worked on between 1926 and 1928, was less successful. Although the Glavrepertkom allowed the Moscow Art Theater to begin production in 1928, it withdrew permission only two weeks after rehearsals began. Such prominent cultural figures as Stanislavsky and Maxim Gorky (the preemiment Soviet writer credited with the creation of the socialist realist literary method) personally begged the censors to reconsider but failed to change their minds, and the play did not find its way to an audience until 1958, when it was staged by the Gorky Theater in provincial Volgograd.

Bulgakov's next two plays, Зойкина квартира (1926) and Багровый остров (1928), were very popular with Moscow theatergoers yet continued to be reviewed negatively by the critical establishment and were taken off the stage after only a few performances. The tightening of Stalin's fist over ideological matters in the late 1920s was accompanied by a pronounced hostility toward the ambivalent political message in Bulgakov's works. Attacks in the press against Bulgakov increased, and by the end of the decade all his plays were banned. By his own reckoning, of the 301 reviews of his work during this period, only three were positive (Wright 145).

By the 1930s, nothing Bulgakov wrote could be published or staged. Not that he was alone in his state-imposed silence. The period was marked by unprecedented repression. Many Russian writers—the life of Anna Akhmatova provides another example of how Stalin's regime treated the country's finest artists—found themselves with no access to the public, their works savagely derided by the censors and denied publication. Those who ventured to speak out against the system often disappeared from their homes in the middle of the night and were not heard from for years; they languished in labor camps or prisons. Millions of people, among them prominent intellectuals and writers such as Isaac Babel, Daniil Kharms, Osip Mandelshtam, and Boris Pilnyak, died in Stalin's purges. All independent artistic groupings were disbanded, and in 1932 a new monolithic institution with no counterpart anywhere in the West, the Union of Soviet Writers, took their place. The union proclaimed there was only one correct way of writing about Soviet reality, socialist realism, and made sure that only works that depicted the triumph of socialist heroes and wholeheartedly praised the new political order would appear in print. Expulsion from the union equaled literary death and often literal death.

Russian writers were faced with difficult choices. Some fully embraced the new socialist realist dogma and benefited from the life of privilege allotted to members of the Writers' Union. Some recanted their previously published but now problematic works publicly in the hope that this self-criticism would spare them—and their family members—the heartache and persecution that were otherwise sure to be their lot. Some chose not to compromise their artistic integrity, even if it meant writing "for the drawer," that is, with the realization that what they produced would be read only in manuscript by a select group, a few friends. Some found partial freedom by writing in such literary genres as satire and science fiction. Still others sought to emigrate.[8]

Unwilling to limit his imagination in any way, Bulgakov fought for his artistic freedom. As early as March 1930, he sent a letter to the Soviet government expressing his concern over the stifling effects of the Party's censorship on creativity in general and drama in particular. As for the personal impasse in which he found himself, he proposed two possible solutions: either he be allowed to return to the theater or be granted permission to emigrate. This act of bravery led to a rather surprising result. Stalin himself telephoned Bulgakov to assure him that his talent was needed at home and that he would be able to work once more. And not surprisingly, soon thereafter he was made assistant director at the Moscow Art Theater, a post he held for the next six years. He described his experiences with the world of the Moscow Art Theater in a scathingly satirical novel, Театральный роман, which was published posthumously in 1966.

The exhilaration following the conversation with Stalin was short-lived, however. For all that he had obtained the job he had longed for, he had not obtained the freedom to practice his art: everything he wrote was found to be too controversial. In the end, the only creative outlet he had left was adaptation.

His play based on Gogol's Мёртвые души was produced in 1932, while his original play Кабала святош

(1929, 1936), about Molière, was banned after only seven performances in 1936 despite enthusiastic public response. Another play, Последние дни (1935), which like the Molière play deals with the theme of the artist struggling for independence but is closer to home in that its subject is Russia's great poet Alexander Pushkin, met with the same end. Two more plays, Блаженство (1934) and Иван Васильевич (1936), were also canceled. Frustrated with what he perceived to be an omnipresent artistic cowardice and hypocrisy and convinced that he had no place in Soviet drama, he moved to the Bolshoi Theater—but left when his works were not produced there either. It was at this time that he accepted the commission to write a play based on *Don Quixote*, but it ran into problems that delayed its production and ultimately prevented its author from seeing it on the stage.

Completely discouraged and seriously ill (a kidney disorder he had inherited from his father led to his untimely death), Bulgakov found the strength to continue work on the novel that was to become his magnum opus: Мастер и Маргарита was produced over a period of twelve years, underwent several revisions, and was completed only weeks before he died in March of 1940. The manuscript was kept by his third wife, Yelena Sergeevna Shilovskaya (the prototype for Margarita) until 1966, when a version abridged by the censors finally appeared in the literary journal Москва. The complete text did not come out until 1973. It secured Bulgakov's place in the pantheon of Russian literature.

Мастер и Маргарита revisits the theme of the artist under an oppressive regime. Its complex narrative structure alternates among three plotlines: the visit of the

Devil to socialist Moscow, during which he and his retinue play jokes of metaphysical importance on Soviet citizens; the Master's fate as a writer whose work does not comply with the dominant ideology and his love for the courageous Margarita; and finally—in a novel within the novel, the novel the Master is writing—the "true" story of Pontius Pilate's encounter with Yeshua Ha-Nozri (Jesus of Nazareth). Impressive as its encyclopedic depiction of Soviet reality is, the novel really deals with a universal theme: the role of the individual in times of ideological and moral crisis. Bulgakov approaches the issue from various angles, most notably through the portrayal of Pilate's cowardice in the face of the creative iconoclasm of Jesus, the account of the Master's failed attempts to publish his controversial manuscript, and the tale of the trials that another artist in the making, Ivan Homeless, must go through to become the Master's spiritual heir. The result is the creation of a Quixotic author-hero through whom Bulgakov redefines such traditional moral categories as courage and honor. Мастер и Маргарита's combination of pathos, sheer creative mastery, and satire offers striking parallels to Cervantes's novel.

Bulgakov, Cervantes, and *Don Quixote*

It was the tragedy of trying to live honorably and courageously and failing that must have attracted Bulgakov, as it attracted many Russian authors before him, to Cervantes's masterpiece. Readers of *Don Quixote* admire its hero's ability to sustain an individualistic vision of the world against contemporary pressure to conform. Although Don Quixote's desire to bring back medieval chivalry is both anachronistic and mad, given seventeenth-century Spain's decisive rejection of feudalism and its ambition to become one of the great powers of Europe, Don Quixote continues to be an admirable figure because of his singular energy and imagination.

Like his hero, Cervantes had to overcome many obstacles to find the proper outlet for his creativity, and the theme of the struggling artist connects his life with that of his hero in a number of ways. Born in 1547 outside Madrid, Miguel de Cervantes Saavedra had a difficult childhood. His father, Rodrigo, was a not particularly successful surgeon, and the family moved often so that he could avoid malpractice suits and jail. This peripatetic life deprived his son of a regular education.

Cervantes began his career as a soldier in the Spanish contingent of the Papal Holy League. The high point in his military service was the defeat of the Ottoman fleet at the Battle of Lepanto in 1571. On his way back to Spain, he was kidnapped by Algerian pirates and held five years for ransom. Released thanks to his parents and the Trinitarian Order, he was welcomed back to Spain as a hero but was unable to translate that status into financial gain.

In the last decades of the sixteenth century Cervantes turned to writing in the hopes that his experiences and talents would secure his family's comfortable existence (he married a much younger woman, Catalina de Salazar y Palacios, in 1584). His first major published work, a pastoral romance called *La Galatea* (1585; the work is named after Galatea, the main character), was unsuccessful. So were his dramatic endeavors: although Spain, like England, had a lively theater scene at the time, Cervantes's plays (of which eight interludes; eight tragicomedies, including *The Commerce of Algiers* [*El trato de Argel*]; and the tragedy *The Siege of Numantia* [*La Numancia*] survive) could not compete with those of the most successful playwright of his day, Félix Lope de Vega. To make ends meet, Cervantes worked as a requisitions officer for the Spanish Armada, a job that led to charges of malfeasance and several jail terms. It was at this low point in his life that he produced the first volume of *Don Quixote* (1605). It became a best seller in Spain and Europe immediately and established his literary career. He would eventually publish *Exemplary Stories* (*Novelas ejemplares* [1613]), *Voyage to Parnassus* (*Viaje del Parnaso* [1614]), *Interludes* (*Entremeses* [1615]), the second volume of *Don Quixote* (1615), and the posthumous *The Travels of Persiles and Sigismunda* (*Los trabajos de Persiles y Sigismunda* [1617]), yet because copyright laws were not yet established anywhere in Europe, he earned little from his works and lived and died on the edge of poverty.[9]

Don Quixote presented Bulgakov with many problems as a source text. Its length is formidable, the two volumes running to over one thousand pages. It derives from and reacts against the highly popular but formulaic chivalric romance, features psychologically complex characters, and gives a comprehensive portrayal of Spanish society—its history, diverse populations, and class structure.

The hero, Alonso Quijano, is an impoverished aristocrat (a hidalgo) who spends more time reading books of chivalry than caring for the family estate. He is about fifty but never married and has no children. His land produces little income because he puts so little effort into it, and he keeps selling off acreage to buy books. Having lost the ability to differentiate between fiction and reality, he styles himself Don Quixote and devises a plan to become a knight-errant and go on the road in search of adventures to right wrongs, restore justice, and bring back the medieval age of chivalry. Three times he leaves home, a small village in the region of La Mancha, looking for adventure, and three times he returns. The first two sallies take place in volume 1, the third in volume 2. Don Quixote makes the first sally on his own; for the second and third he persuades his neighbor, Sancho Panza, a peasant, to join him. His return to sanity toward the end of the novel is spurred by a series of losses, the first of which is his defeat in a joust by Sansón Carrasco, a fellow villager. Fully cured, he rejects chivalric romances and his adventures as Don Quixote, puts his affairs in order, and dies.

Cervantes had the luxury of a lengthy novel to develop Quixote's character and explore his relation to the world, but Bulgakov, tied to the economies of the stage, had to compress the material to accommodate an evening at the theater. The result is a four-act play with a smaller scope of action. Whereas Cervantes includes stories of a variety of characters, both major and minor, as well as many interpolated tales, Bulgakov's drama focuses on Don Quixote, cutting the number of adventures significantly and narrowing their scope. For instance, the proceedings at the Duke and Duchess's estate dominate volume 2 of the novel, but Bulgakov preserves only Don Quixote's discussion with the priest, Sancho's argument with the *dueña* Doña Rodríguez, and Sancho's claim to the governorship of the island. He hollows out the characters of the Duke and Duchess to allow Sansón Carrasco to make a clean and simple entry, challenge Don Quixote, win the joust, and take him home. Cervantes's portrayal of the Duke and Duchess in the novel represents an indictment of the decadent ruling class and its misuse of authority. Bulgakov's reduction of them creates a void that would seem to avert attention from the question of the abuses of power and its connection to his own society, but that void accomplishes the opposite: it highlights the inexorable presence in the play of the Soviet state.

Bulgakov concentrates on Quixote's interaction with Sancho Panza, with women, with the common folk, with the wealthy, with the educated, and with the clergy. As in the novel, the Don Quixote–Sancho relationship is primary. Act 1 is devoted to the dramatic development of their characters. Of the adventures that constitute the first sally in the novel, Bulgakov chooses only the famous windmill episode, using it to establish the relationship between the two men. In the novel, Sancho often raises the issue of Don Quixote's sanity, but in the play his fundamental concern is with Don Quixote's well-being. The squire never waivers in his trust in his master's narrative. The friendship that develops between them at the beginning of the play acquires special importance (and provides a nice structural frame in the adaptation) toward the end, in scene 9, when we see the two once again by themselves on the stage after Don Quixote's defeat at the hands of Carrasco. In this, the most intimate moment in the play, Don Quixote reveals his private thoughts and shares with Sancho his insights about the meaning of life. Sancho not only provides comfort but also reinforces the value of the pursuit of idealism.

A key element of the chivalric code is the knight's platonic relationship with women. This theme happens to dovetail with a turn to more conservative morals in the Stalinist era (compared with the early years of the

Revolution). Chaste depictions of relationships are found in many films and books of the 1930s. Bulgakov makes use of this point of contact between the original work and the cultural context of his play to mark the transition from volume 1 to volume 2 of the novel. In Cervantes, Don Quixote initiates his own story in volume 1; in volume 2, other characters create the chivalric fictions, in which he is only a player. Although Cervantes gives his hero numerous opportunities to interact with women, Bulgakov concentrates on Antonia (the niece) and Aldonza Lorenzo (Dulcinea). Aldonza's appearance in scene 1 of the play instigates Quijano's creation of the Don Quixote narrative. In act 2, scene 5, it is the Barber, the Priest, and the Niece (in the role of the damsel in distress) who produce the rescue scenario to lure the wandering knight back home.

If the master-squire interactions underscore the importance of friendship and loyalty and if the female characters illustrate the success or failure of Don Quixote's enactment of the chivalric code, representatives of the lower classes demonstrate the real-world effects of his obsessions. Cervantes's hero causes chaos wherever he might be—on the road, at an inn, in the mountains. Bulgakov compresses the chaos theme into two scenes: in act 1, scene 2, Don Quixote's hubris produces uncontrollable violence in the encounter with the twelve Yanguesan mule drivers; in act 2, a balm that is meant to restore his health after the beating results in the mass diarrhea of the customers at the inn. There is an important difference in Bulgakov's treatment of the nature of the disorder that accompanies Don Quixote's actions: Cervantes makes Don Quixote solely responsible for the turmoil; Bulgakov attributes the responsibility for the chaos to the collective. The Yanguesans are drunk and unable to act with restraint in the face of what to them seems a ridiculous challenge. The innkeeper and his guests insist on using the balm that Don Quixote intended only for himself (in the novel, only Sancho Panza and Don Quixote swallow the concoction). Note that Bulgakov assigns a practical value to the balm: as the mule driver at the inn points out, it can be used as an animal purgative. Bulgakov thus blurs the line between the imaginary and the real. Don Quixote's imaginary miracle cure for wounded knights turns into an actual medicine for livestock.

Don Quixote suffers physically at the hands of the lower classes, but they do not affect his emotional and psychological well-being. Not until he clashes with the upper classes and the educated does he begin to lose control over his identity. Bulgakov follows Cervantes's lead here. In both the novel and the play, Don Quixote initially encounters commoners who may react to him but leave him free to follow his vision. With the appearance of Carrasco and the Duke and Duchess, who see that the source of his madness is chivalry, he is vulnerable and can be manipulated. If in the Duke and Duchess Bulgakov condemns the decadence of the ruling class, his view of the intelligentsia as represented by Sansón Carrasco is more nuanced. Carrasco brings Don Quixote home literally but also metaphorically, as the return to the village is marked by a return to sanity. On a more symbolic level, the relationship between Carrasco and Don Quixote introduces a theme of vital importance to the author of Мастер и Маргарита: the betrayal of a fellow intellectual. For this theme Bulgakov abandons his usual strategy of compression and significantly expands Carrasco's presence in the play.

One other group that both the novel and the play deal with is religious figures. Throughout the novel, Don Quixote encounters penitents, friars, and priests. Because the penitents and friars are commoners, their dealings with him result only in temporary disorder, but the priests engage him intellectually, arguing with him about his chosen path. Bulgakov minimizes the presence of religious figures. The Benedictine friars in act 1, scene 2, grace the stage only briefly and have no lines. But when in act 3, scene 6, a priest upbraids Don Quixote for letting his imagination run away with him and instructs him, "вернитесь в свой дом, учите ваших детей," Don Quixote responds with what may be the most powerful speech in the play:

> Имейте в виду, что только то, что я нахожусь в гостях у герцога, да еще ваш сан сдерживают мою ярость, иначе вам пришлось бы плохо. Ну что же, я буду сражаться с вами вашим оружием — языком. Скажите мне, за какое именно из моих безумств вы осуждаете меня больше всего и приказываете мне учить детей, которых у меня никогда не было? Вы считаете, что человек, странствующий по свету не в поисках наслаждений, а в поисках терний, безумен и праздно тратит время? Люди выбирают разные пути. Один, спотыкаясь, карабкается по дороге тщеславия, другой ползет по тропе унизительной лести, иные пробираются по дороге лицемерия и обмана. Иду ли я по одной из этих дорог? Нет! Я иду по крутой дороге рыцарства и презираю земные блага, но не честь! За кого я мстил, вступая в бой с гигантами, которые вас так раздражили?

> Я заступался за слабых, обиженных сильными! Если я видел где-нибудь зло, я шел на смертельную схватку, чтобы побить чудовищ злобы и преступлений! Вы их не видите нигде? У вас плохое зрение, святой отец! Моя цель светла — всем сделать добро и никому не причинить зла. И за это я, по-вашему, заслуживаю порицания? Если бы меня сочли сумасшедшим рыцари, я был бы оскорблен до глубины души, но ваши слова я не ставлю ни в грош, они мне кажутся смешными!

The priest wants him to return to a life of conformity, but Don Quixote argues passionately in defense of his vision. Bulgakov's hero stresses the validity of his choice, contrasting it with other, less daring, and morally suspect paths. In the context of life under Stalin with all its incumbent compromises, this speech acquires a pointedness that any Soviet citizen would have recognized. In Don Quixote's defense of his choice, Bulgakov underscores the need to pursue one's art without conceding to institutions of authority—that is, without giving in to Party directives. By putting these words into Don Quixote's mouth, he grounds the play in its historical moment.

In the corresponding speech from the novel (vol. 2, ch. 32), Cervantes rather daringly has Don Quixote explode with anticlerical barbs that amount to a spirited attack against the church, a scathing criticism of its dominance in Spanish life. Bulgakov redirects the focus of Don Quixote's words from the social critique of oppressive institutions to the moral imperative of individuals to be true to themselves. Taking this high road, Don Quixote emerges the victor, and the priest exits, never to return.

One group of characters very much present in the novel is conspicuous by its absence in the play: government officials. In the novel, Don Quixote and Sancho encounter many soldiers and members of the Holy Brotherhood, the judicial police force created by Ferdinand and Isabel to restore royal authority throughout Spain after the *Reconquista*. The wandering knight attracts the attention of the law especially in volume 1, and by the end of the volume a warrant for his arrest has been issued. Given the realities of Soviet police control over life in Russia in the 1930s, it is understandable that Bulgakov chose to avoid episodes that might have been interpreted as references to the very real fears of the Soviet people. The key to understanding the adaptation lies not so much in the visible, what Bulgakov includes of the novel's main narrative preoccupations, as in the invisible, what he leaves unsaid.

Bulgakov's Дон Кихот

At the end of act 4, scene 8, the Duke and Carrasco remain alone on the stage after the defeated Don Quixote is carried off by Sancho and pages. The two drop their masks and confront each other's very different ideologies. The Duke sees what has just transpired as a joke and complains that it has gone too far. The serious consequences of the joust have marred his amusement, and he holds Carrasco responsible. Carrasco's problem is with the Duke and people like him, who exploit Don Quixote and reduce him to entertainment. On the surface their argument is about opposing visions of the Don, exploitative versus compassionate. But the vigilant reader might uncover another level of significance in the scene, one that connects it with both the work's immediate cultural context and the author's major thematic concerns.

When Carrasco enters the Duke's estate as the Knight of the White Moon, the Duke simply assumes that he will become part of the entertainment. Instead Carrasco challenges the Duke's control over the Don Quixote script and takes his toy away. He is even so bold as to criticize the Duke's behavior and suggest that there are natural-born clowns who could better serve as jesters in his court than a man like Don Quixote, who doesn't deserve such treatment ("и нужно ли для развлечения рядить в шуты, увеличивая число шутов природных, человека, который этого совершенно не заслуживает?"). Yet when the Duke challenges Carrasco's moral imperative, Carrasco backs down ("Я не настолько дерзок, чтобы осмелиться вас учить. Считайте, что я рассуждаю сам с собой") and exits, leaving the dominant power structure intact. Thus Carrasco as a version of the creative artist (he fashions the Knight of the White Moon narrative, inspired by love, just as Quijano formulates his knightly identity, inspired by his adoration of Dulcinea) betrays himself and his kind. He is a kindhearted coward but a coward nevertheless. Throughout Bulgakov's work cowardice is a great sin (the gravest in Мастер и Маргарита) and one from which the Soviet intelligentsia tends to suffer.

Because of his cowardice, Carrasco cannot fully appreciate Don Quixote's courage to act on his imagination, so all his compassion comes to naught. His vision of Don Quixote is too much like the priest's: he wants him to go home to an ordinary, banal existence. In the play as in Мастер и Маргарита, Bulgakov's ultimately tragic conclusion is that the true artist can never find a place for himself in Soviet life. Death is the only way out. As Don Quixote watches the sunset in act 4, scene 9 (he has recovered his senses at this point), he realizes that the life he has chosen is slipping away, but he welcomes the darkness and awaits death with calm anticipation, even love: "И вот она пришла за мной. Я ей рад." A life of normalcy has nothing of value to offer the artist. Bulgakov revisits this theme in the final chapters of Мастер и Маргарита. The Master, the ultimate artist, begs for and is granted a peaceful existence in eternal darkness, in death. When in 1938, gravely ill, Bulgakov was working on both these texts, he could sense the nearing of his own end. The public concern with the fate of the creative individual thus acquires an additional, private resonance for him. Processing and assessing the ends of Don Quixote and the Master is a way of processing and assessing his own death.

The reflection of Soviet reality makes itself felt in Bulgakov's interpretation of the source text in the highly innovative ways in which the playwright tackles the question of community. Cervantes's Don Quixote has often been interpreted as an avatar of individualism (Watt xiv), and as such he is alienated from the other characters. Bulgakov counters the view of Don Quixote as the suffering, solitary individual by integrating him into the people and situations he encounters. Simply put, Bulgakov returns Don Quixote to the community. In so doing, he is allegorically evaluating both the positive and negative aspects of life in the Soviet collective.

The opening scene is as much an introduction to the village as it is to the main character. Bulgakov's hero is always part of an ensemble: he is almost never alone on stage, and characters are always rushing to his side, even crowding him with their presence. The scene at the inn is an example. The hectic activity on- and offstage turns into chaos, but out of the hurly-burly emerges a Don Quixote whose value to the community is recognized.

Yet the integration of Don Quixote into the collective comes at a high price: the only way society can assimilate the chaos in a meaningful way is if his vision is controlled by the many. The villagers' commitment to a life of normalcy translates into a desire to overpower that vision. This desire is expressed most clearly in an episode cut from the final version. In the earlier version of act 2, scene 4, Bulgakov presents the Niece, the Barber, the Housekeeper, and the Priest during a rehearsal of their prospective meeting with Don Quixote. Each takes a turn at being (performing) Don Quixote. The symbolic appropriation of the artist's existence illustrates the gravest danger that collective life poses to the individual: peaceful coexistence with the social fold can weaken one's imagination. In this context, theater becomes synonymous with art as propaganda.

Concern about the misappropriation of art, about its use as an instrument for ideological suppression, is the reason why Bulgakov makes so much of the play within the play, which he invents out of whole cloth: it does not exist in the novel. The scene was cut from the final version of Дон Кихот ostensibly because of running time issues, but one has to wonder whether anxiety about the censors' response might not have led to the scene's omission.

The communal existence of the individual in Bulgakov's Russia also translates into a peculiar character doubling, which brings together Don Quixote and Sansón Carrasco in a creative way. The two knights have more in common in the play than in the novel. Carrasco is the only character who understands and sympathizes with Don Quixote's ideals. The two are also physically alike, and in the final scene they both appear with one arm in a sling, which suggests that Bulgakov intended to present them as mirror images. In addition, both are already doubled: Don Quixote is Alonso Quijano, and Carrasco is the Knight of the White Moon. They differ, however, in the way they use their fictive selves. For Don Quixote the fiction becomes reality, determining his sense of self and the path in life he has chosen. For Carrasco the fictive identity is duplicitous, designed to fool others. The educated bachelor of arts may represent a version of Don Quixote's artist, but once he dons the costume of the Knight of the White Moon and with it the theatrical persona of a false knight, he becomes an other to himself and Don Quixote alike. True, by saving the Knight of the Doleful Countenance from the clutches of the Duke and Duchess, he acts nobly, as a knight should; yet by acting like his fellow villagers, he too wishes to control Don Quixote's chosen identity and transform Don Quixote into a safe, predictable citizen who has internalized the accepted values of the community.

The unstable, even contradictory allegiances of Carrasco complicate his character in ways that draw attention to the ethical responsibility of the self to the other. Ultimately, he, much like Pilate from Мастер и Маргарита, recognizes the futility of his power over his adversary and suffers from profound guilt. Although he may not fully recognize the value of the artistic freedom he has helped expunge from Don Quixote, his remorse allows Quijano to realize, as Quijano throws off the Don Quixote persona and prepares to die, that something important is now missing from their world. Carrasco's last words and the words that bring the play to a close, "Я сделать больше ничего не могу. Он мертв," link his own existence, as well as the existence of the community as a whole, with Don Quixote. The end of Don Quixote signals their end as well.

Cervantes does not conclude his novel with Don Quixote's passing. That the village goes on following a short period of mourning and that Don Quixote is all but forgotten reinforce the author's view of his hero as a solitary, alienated individual. In Bulgakov, the collective without Don Quixote loses its vibrancy. A society without an artist can accomplish nothing.

Bulgakov's adaptation, then, should be viewed as more than a repetition of Cervantes's text. It is an independent work of creative power and thematic focus, especially when read together with Мастер и Маргарита.[10] Repression never really works: the famous epigram to the novel about the devil's always willing evil and always producing good, which Bulgakov borrowed from Goethe,[11] is relevant to the play. The identity of the imaginative artist transcends death in both works. The Master and Don Quixote alike find the peace they have so longed for without compromising the integrity of their vision. Both also inspire the love and admiration of those among their fellow citizens who recognize their abilty to rise above a degrading authoritarian world.

That Bulgakov understood the fine line between good and evil made him the ideal interpreter of the role of the artist in the Soviet world.

Notes

[1] A detailed exploration of Bulgakov's attitude toward the play and of his personal struggles while writing it can be found in Curtis 255–77.

[2] He had already played Don Quixote twice, in L. F. Minkus's ballet of the same name and in Alexandra Brushtein's musical comedy version, and was to reprise his role in the 1957 Russian film version of *Don Quixote* directed by Grigory Kozintsev (Wright 240).

[3] A comprehensive introduction to the history of Cervantes's novel in Russia can be found in Turkevich.

[4] For more information, see Esipova.

[5] Smirnova confirms this point when she writes of Bulgakov's play, "так много вложено в неё автором своих мыслей чувств, так много отдано самого себя обоим героям" (331).

[6] Stalin made travel beyond the borders of the motherland a virtual impossibility for its citizens, who were required to apply to the government for permission to go abroad for any reason.

[7] For excellent overviews of the different types of popular drama during Stalin's regime, see Rudnitsky; Segel.

[8] For more detailed discussion of the issues facing Soviet writers during this time, see Dobrenko; Garrard and Garrard.

[9] For more detailed information about Cervantes's life see Byron; McKendrick; and Canavaggio.

[10] For Doyle the play presents a "fascinating example of [Bulgakov's] ability to reinterpret and transcend his source material and so to create a distinctively personal and topical work" (877). Esipova finds that "[в] концу работы над пьесой писатель ощущал её как собственное важнейшее 'слово'" (104).

[11] In Goethe's *Faust*, part 1, scene 3, Mephistopheles introduces himself to Faust as "Part of that Power, not understood, / Which always wills the Bad, and always works the Good."

Works Cited

Bulgakov, Mikhail. Мастер и Маргарита. Biblioteka Vekhi, 2001. Web. 6 Jan. 2014. <http://vehi.net/mbulgakov/master/>.

Byron, William. *Cervantes: A Biography*. Garden City: Doubleday, 1978. Print.

Canavaggio, Jean. *Cervantes*. New York: Norton, 1990. Print.

Cervantes Saavedra, Miguel de. *Don Quixote*. Trans. Edith Grossman. New York: Ecco, 2003. Print.

Curtis, A. E. *Manuscripts Don't Burn: Mikhail Bulgakov: A Life in Letters and Diaries*. London: Bloomsbury, 1991. Print.

Dobrenko, Evgeny. *The Making of the State Writer: Social and Aesthetic Origins of Soviet Literary Culture*. Trans. Jesse Savage. Stanford: Stanford UP, 2001. Print.

Doyle, Peter. "Bulgakov and Cervantes." *Modern Language Review* 78 (1983): 867–77. Print.

Esipova, O. E. "О пьесе М. Булгакова 'Дон Кихот.'" Проблемы театрального наследия М. А. Булгакова. Leningrad: LGIT-Mik, 1987. 87–104. Print.

Garrard, John, and Carol Garrard. *Inside the Soviet Writers' Union*. London: Tauris, 1990. Print.

Goethe, Wolfgang von. *Faust*. Trans. Bayard Taylor. New York: Modern Lib., 1967. Print.

McKendrick, Melveena. *Cervantes*. Boston: Little, 1980. Print.

Rudnitsky, Konstantin. *Russian and Soviet Theater: Tradition and the Avant-Garde*. Trans. Roxane Permar. London: Thames, 1988. Print.

Segel, Harold B. *Twentieth-Century Russian Drama: From Gorky to the Present*. New York: Columbia UP, 1979. Print.

Smirnova, V. V. "Михаил Булгаков — драматург." Современный портрет: Статьи. Moscow: Sovetskij pisatel', 1964. 282–332. Print.

Turkevich, Ludmilla. *Cervantes in Russia*. Princeton: Princeton UP, 1950. Print.

Watt, Ian P. *Myths of Modern Individualism: Faust, Don Quixote, Don Juan, Robinson Crusoe*. Cambridge: Cambridge UP, 1996. Print.

Wright, A. Collin. *Mikhail Bulgakov: Life and Interpretations*. Toronto: U of Toronto P, 1978. Print.

Selected Bibliography of Works by and about Mikhail Bulgakov

Anisimov, I. "'Дон Кихот' в театре Вахтангова." Советское исскуство 27 Apr. 1941: 3. Print.

Belozerskaya-Bulgakova, Lyubov. *My Life with Mikhail Bulgakov*. New York: Ardis, 1983. Print.

Bulgakov, Mikhail. *Bulgakov: Six Plays*. Trans. Michael Glenny and Michael Earley. London: Methuen, 1991. Print.

———. *"Diaboliad" and Other Stories*. Trans. Carl Proffer. Bloomington: Indiana UP, 1972. Print.

———. *A Dog's Heart: An Appalling Story*. Trans. Andrew Bromfield. New York: Penguin Books, 2007. Print.

———. Дон Кихот. Letchworth-Herts: Prideaux, 1971. Print. Russian Studies for the Specialist 23.

———. *The Fatal Eggs*. Trans. Hugh Aplin. London: Hesperus, 2005. Print.

———. Flight *and* Bliss: *Two Plays*. Trans. Mirra Ginsburg. New York: New Directions, 1985. Print.

———. *The Master and Margarita*. Trans. Michael Glenny. London: Collins, 1967. Print.

———. *The Master and Margarita*. Trans. Richard Pevear and Larissa Volokhonsky. New York: Penguin, 1997. Print.

———. "Неизданные сцены из пьесы 'Дон Кихот.'" Сервантес и всемирная литература. Ed. N. I. Balashov. Moscow: Nauka, 1969. 273–77. Print.

———. Неизвестный Булгаков. Ed. Viktor Losev. Moscow: Knižnaja palata, 1993. Print.

———. *"Notes on the Cuff" and Other Stories*. Trans. Alison Rice. New York: Ardis, 1991. Print.

———. Собрание сочинений в десяти томах. Ed. Viktor Petelin. Moscow: Golos, 1995. Print.

———. Собрание сочинений в восьми томах. Ed. V. I. Losev. Saint Petersburg: Azbuka-klassika, 2002. Print.

———. *The White Guard*. Trans. Marian Schwartz. New Haven: Yale UP, 2008. Print.

Chudakova, M. O. "К творческой биографии М. Булгакова, 1916–23 (По материалам архива писателя)." Вопросы литературы 7 (1973): 231–55. Print.

Curtis, A. E. *Manuscripts Don't Burn: Mikhail Bulgakov: A Life in Letters and Diaries*. London: Bloomsbury, 1991. Print.

Ermolinskii, Sergei. "О Михаиле Булгакове." Театр 9 Sept. 1966: 79–97. Print.

Esipova, O. E. "О пьесе М. Булгакова 'Дон Кихот.'" Проблемы театрального наследия М. А. Булгакова. Leningrad: LGITMik, 1987. 87–104. Print.

Haber, Edythe C. *Mikhail Bulgakov: The Early Years*. Cambridge: Harvard UP, 1998. Print.

Milne, Lesley. *Bulgakov: The Novelist-Playwright*. London: Routledge, 1996. Print. Russian Theatre Archive.

Proffer, Ellendea. *Mikhail Bulgakov*. Ann Arbor: Ardis, 1978. Print.

Smeliansky, Anatoly. *Is Comrade Bulgakov Dead? Mikhail Bulgakov at the Moscow Art Theatre*. Trans. Arch Tait. London: Routledge, 1993. Print.

———. Михаил Булгаков в Художественном Театре. Moscow: Iskusstvo, 1989. Print.

Varlamov, Aleksei. Михаил Булгаков. Moscow: Molodaja gvardija, 2008. Print.

Weeks, Laura, ed. Master and Margarita*: A Critical Companion*. Chicago: Northwestern UP, 1996. Print.

Wright, A. Collin. *Mikhail Bulgakov: Life and Interpretations*. Toronto: U of Toronto P, 1978. Print.

Zavalishin, V. *Early Soviet Writers.* New York: Praeger, 1958. Print.

SUGGESTIONS FOR FURTHER READING

Bradshaw, Martha, ed. *Soviet Theaters, 1917–1941*. New York: Research Program on the USSR, 1954. Print.

Byron, William. *Cervantes: A Biography*. Garden City: Doubleday, 1978. Print.

Canavaggio, Jean. *Cervantes*. New York: Norton, 1990. Print.

Cascardi, Anthony J. *The Bounds of Reason: Cervantes, Dostoevsky, Flaubert*. New York: Columbia UP, 1986. Print.

Davies, Sarah, and James Harris, eds. *Stalin: A New History*. Cambridge: Cambridge UP, 2006. Print.

Dobrenko, Evgeny. *The Making of the State Writer: Social and Aesthetic Origins of Soviet Literary Culture*. Trans. Jesse Savage. Stanford: Stanford UP, 2001. Print.

Finch, Patricia, and John Jay Allen. "*Don Quijote* across the Centuries." Don Quijote*: A New Translation, Backgrounds and Contexts, Criticism*. Ed. Diana de Armas Wilson. Trans. Burton Raffel. New York: Norton, 1999. 767–74. Print.

Garrard, John, and Carol Garrard. *Inside the Soviet Writers' Union*. London: Tauris, 1990. Print.

Gorchakov, N. A. *The Theater in Soviet Russia*. Trans. Edgar Lehrman. New York: Columbia UP, 1957. Print.

Kemp-Welch, A. *Stalin and the Literary Intelligentsia, 1928–39.* New York: Palgrave-Macmillan, 1991. Print.

Mancing, Howard. *The Cervantes Encyclopedia.* Westport: Greenwood, 2004. Print.

McKendrick, Melveena. *Cervantes.* Boston: Little, 1980. Print.

Rasula, Jed. "When Exception Is the Rule: *Don Quixote* as Incitement to Literature." *Comparative Literature* 51.2 (1999): 123–51. Print.

Rudnitsky, Konstantin. *Russian and Soviet Theater: Tradition and the Avant-Garde.* Trans. Roxane Permar. London: Thames, 1988. Print.

Segel, Harold B. *Twentieth-Century Russian Drama: From Gorky to the Present.* New York: Columbia UP, 1979. Print.

Slonim, M. *Soviet Russian Literature: Writers and Problems.* New York: Oxford, 1969. Print.

Struve, Gleb. *Russian Literature under Lenin and Stalin.* London: Routledge, 1972. Print.

Tucker, Robert. *Stalin in Power: The Revolution from Above, 1928–1941.* New York: Norton, 1992. Print.

Turkevich, Ludmilla. *Cervantes in Russia.* Princeton: Princeton UP, 1950. Print.

NOTE ON THE TEXT

The Russian text is in the public domain. This volume uses the 1971 edition of the play, Дон Кихот: Пьеса, published in *Russian Studies for the Specialist* 23, by the Prideaux Press. It is a faithful and complete reproduction of the work that Bulgakov finished in December 1938.

Михаил Булгаков.

Дон Кихот.

Пьеса по Сервантесу в четырех действиях,
девяти картинах

ДЕЙСТВУЮЩИЕ ЛИЦА

Алонсо Кихано, он же Дон Кихот Ламанчский.
Антония — его племянница.
Ключница Дон Кихота.
Санчо Панса — оруженосец Дон Кихота.
Перо Перес — деревенский священник, лиценциат.
Николас — деревенский цирюльник.
Альдонса Лоренсо — крестьянка.
Сансон Карраско — бакалавр.
Паломек Левша — хозяин постоялого двора.
Мариторнес — служанка на постоялом дворе.
Погонщик мулов

Тенорио Эрнандес	постояльцы Паломека.
Педро Мартинес	
Слуга Мартинеса	

Работник на постоялом дворе.
Герцог.
Герцогиня.
Духовник Герцога.
Мажордом Герцога.
Доктор Агуэро.
Дуэнья Родригес.
Паж Герцога.
Свиновод.
Женщина.
Первый и Второй старики.
Первый и Второй монахи.
Первый и Второй слуги.
Погонщики лошадей.
Свита Герцога.

Действие происходит в Испании в самом конце XVI века.

ДЕЙСТВИЕ ПЕРВОЕ

КАРТИНА ПЕРВАЯ

Летний вечер. Двор дома Дон Кихота с конюшней, колодцем, скамейкой и двумя калитками: одной — на заднем плане, выводящей на дорогу, и другой — сбоку, ведущей в деревню. Кроме того, внутренность дома Дон Кихота. В комнате Дон Кихота большая кровать за пологом, кресло, стол, старые рыцарские доспехи и множество книг.[1]

Николас (*с цирюльными принадлежностями появляется во дворе.*). Сеньора ключница! Нету ее? (*Поднимается в дом, стучится.*) Сеньор Кихано, можно войти? Сеньор Кихано!.. Видно, никого нет. (*Входит в комнату Дон Кихота.*) Сеньора племянница!.. Куда

References to Cervantes's novel are formatted in this way: Cervantes 1.1 means volume 1, chapter 1, of *Don Quixote*.

[1] Cervantes 1.1. Don Quixote has an extensive library of romances—that is, medieval narratives in prose or verse relating the heroic exploits of knights-errant. In Cervantes, Don Quixote is so obsessed with this reading matter that he has sold acreage from his estate to pay for the books.

же это они все девались? А велел прийти стричь! Ну что же, подожду, благо спешить мне некуда. (*Ставит цирюльный тазик на стол, обращает внимание на рыцарские доспехи.*) Скажи пожалуйста, какая вещь! Откуда же он все это взял? А, знаю, эти латы он с чердака снял. Чудак! (*Садится, берет со стола книгу, читает.*) Зер-ка-ло ры-цар-ства...[2] Гм... До чего он любит этих рыцарей, уму непостижимо...

Дон Кихот (*за сценой*). Бернардо дель Карпио! Бернардо дель Карпио![3]

Николас. Его голос? Его. Он идет. (*Высовывается в окно.*)

Дон Кихот (*за сценой*). Великий Бернардо дель Карпио задушил в Ронсевале очарованного дон Роланда!..[4]

Николас (*в окне.*) Что это он плетет?

---

[2] First published between 1533 and 1554, the *Mirror of Knighthood* is a Spanish prose adaptation of Boiardo's *Orlando innamorato* ("Orlando in Love").

[3] Cervantes most likely refers to the poem by Agustín Alonso, *Historia de las hazañas y hechos del invincible caballero Bernardo del Carpio* (1585; "History of the Exploits and Deeds of the Invincible Knight Bernardo del Carpio"), a key text in the tradition of the chivalric romance. Russian audiences would not have recognized its importance, but they would have appreciated the Spanish flavor of the reference.

[4] Roland, a famous knight, is the chief peer under Charlemagne and the hero of the oldest surviving major work in French literature, *The Song of Roland* (1040–1115). The culminating battle in that work occurs at Roncesvalles, a mountain pass between France and Spain.

Дон Кихот (*появляется через калитку на заднем плане с книгой в одной руке и с мечом в другой*). Ах, если бы мне, рыцарю Дон Кихоту Ламанчскому, в наказание за смертные мои грехи или в награду за то доброе, что я совершил в моей жизни, пришлось бы наконец встретиться с тем, кого я ищу! Ах!..

Николас. Какому Дон Кихоту? Эге-ге, да с ним, кажется, неладно!

Дон Кихот. Да, если бы мне довелось встретиться с врагом моим — великаном Брандабарбараном в змеиной коже...[5]

Николас. Брандабар... Да наш идальго окончательно спятил?!

Дон Кихот. ... я последовал бы примеру Бернардо. Подняв великана, я задушил бы его в воздухе! (*Отбрасывает книгу и начинает рубить воздух мечом.*)

Николас. Праведное небо!

Дон Кихот поднимается в дом, Николас прячется за рыцарские доспехи.

---

[5] Cervantes 1.18. The name *Brandabarbarán de Boliche* has a meaning in thieves' cant: the gambling hall of a brothel. It comes from an omitted scene in which Don Quixote and Sancho encounter two herds of sheep that Don Quixote perceives as warring Christian and Muslim armies. The names and descriptions he produces for the knights are fanciful and farcical, grounded neither in history nor in published chivalric romances. Bulgakov probably liked the name because of its comic potential.

Дон Кихот. Здесь кто-то есть?.. Кто здесь?

Николас. Это я, милейший сеньор Кихано, это я...

Дон Кихот. А, наконец-то судьба осчастливила меня встречей с тобой, мой кровный враг! Выходи же сюда, не прячься в тени!

Николас. Помилосердствуйте, сеньор Кихано, что вы говорите! Какой я вам враг!

Дон Кихот. Не притворяйся, чары твои предо мной бессильны! Я узнаю тебя: ты — лукавый волшебник Фристон![6]

Николас. Сеньор Алонсо, придите в себя, умоляю вас! Всмотритесь в черты моего лица, я не волшебник, я цирюльник, ваш верный друг и кум Николас![7]

Дон Кихот. Ты лжешь!

Николас. Помилуйте!..

Дон Кихот. Выходи на бой со мною!

Николас. О, горе мне, он не слушает меня. Сеньор Алонсо, опомнитесь! Перед вами христианская душа, а вовсе не волшебник! Оставьте ваш страшный меч, сеньор!

Дон Кихот. Бери оружие и выходи!

Николас. Ангел-хранитель, помоги мне!.. (*Выскакивает в окно и выбегает через боковую калитку.*)

---

[6] In the novel, Don Quixote names Frestón the Magician as his primary antagonist, blaming him for the disappearance of his library, the enchantment of Dulcinea, and other misadventures.

[7] Кум is a dated form of addressing an elder.

Дон Кихот успокаивается, садится, раскрывает книгу. За оградой прошел кто-то, зазвенели струны, и тяжелый бас пропел:[8]

Ах, краса твоя, без спора,
Ярче солнечного дня!
Где же ты, моя сеньора?
Иль забыла ты меня?

Альдонса (*входит во двор с корзиной в руках*). Сеньора ключница, а сеньора ключница!..

Дон Кихот. Чей голос слышу я? Неужели опять меня смущает колдун?.. Это она!

Альдонса. Сеньора ключница, вы дома? (*Оставляет свою корзину внизу, поднимается в дом, стучится.*)

Дон Кихот. Это она стучит? Нет, нет, стучит мое сердце!

Альдонса (*входит*). Ах! Простите, почтеннейший сеньор, я не знала, что вы здесь. Это я, Альдонса Лоренсо. Вашей ключницы нет дома? Я принесла соленую свинину и оставила ее внизу, в кухне.

Дон Кихот. Вы появились вовремя, сеньора. Я отправляюсь в путь для встречи с великаном

[8] The bass voice was particularly important in nineteenth- and early-twentieth-century Russian opera. Fyodor Chaliapine (1873–1938), the most famous Russian bass, played Don Quixote in G. W. Pabst's film adaptation *The Adventures of Don Quixote* (1933).

Каракулиамбро,[9] повелителем острова Мамендрания. Я хочу победить его и прислать к вам с тем, чтобы он упал перед вами на колени, и просил бы вас распорядиться им по вашему желанию...

Альдонса. Ах, сударь, что вы говорите, помилуй нас господи!

Дон Кихот. Я хочу, чтобы он рассказал вам, как произошло его столкновение с Дон Кихотом Ламанчским... Знайте, безжалостная, что этот Дон Кихот перед вами!

Альдонса. Сеньор Кихано, зачем вы стали на колени?! Я просто не знаю, что и делать...

Дон Кихот. Каракулиамбро расскажет вам, как было дело. А было так... (*Берет книгу и начинает читать.*) "Лишь только румянощекий Аполлон разбросал по земле нити своих золотых волос, а златотронная Аврора поднялась с пуховиков своего ревнивого супруга..."[10]

---

[9] Cervantes 1.1. The giant's name is slightly obscene—*cara* ("face"), *culo* ("ass").

[10] Cervantes 1.2. In both the book and the play, Don Quixote leaves the village for his first adventure by himself, although Bulgakov's text begins in media res—that is, after Don Quixote has returned from the initial adventure. In the play, he reads a quotation from a romance; in the novel, he imagines how a historian will write about his departure and produces the lines quoted above out of his own imagination—that is, he creates the lines instead of quoting them.

Альдонса. Перестаньте, сеньор, прошу вас! Я простая девушка, но и мне не пристало слушать такие речи...

Дон Кихот (*читает*). "В это время Дон Белианис сел на своего коня и тронулся в путь..."[11] (*Берет меч.*)

Альдонса. Побегу, скажу ключнице... (*Бесшумно скрывается.*)

Дон Кихот. Я заменяю имя Белианиса именем Дон Кихота... Дон Кихот отправился навстречу опасностям и мукам с одной мыслью о вас, владычица моя, о Дульсинея из Тобосо! (*Оглядывается.*) Исчезла! Угас блистающий луч! Значит, меня посетило видение? Зачем же, зачем ты, поманив, покинула меня? Кто похитил тебя? И вновь я один, и мрачные волшебные тени обступают меня. Прочь! Я не боюсь вас! (*Поражает воздух мечом, потом успокаивается, берет книгу, садится, читает, бормочет что-то.*)

Сумерки. За оградой послышался тихий таинственный свист. Над оградой показывается голова Санчо Панса. Санчо свистит еще раз, потом голова его скрывается. Санчо входит во двор, ведя в поводу своего серого осла, нагруженного бурдюком и вьюками.

---

[11] The eponymous character from the romance of chivalry *Belianís de Grecia*.

Санчо привязывает осла, тревожно оглядывается, поднимается по лестнице и входит в комнату Дон Кихота, предварительно еще раз свистнув.

Санчо. Сударь...

Дон Кихот. А! Ты опять появился, неугомонный чародей? Ну, теперь ты не уйдешь! Сдавайся!

Санчо (*став на колени*). Сдаюсь.

Дон Кихот (*приставив острие меча ко лбу Санчо*). Наконец-то ты в моей власти, презренный колдун!

Санчо. Сеньор! Протрите свои глаза, прежде чем выколоть мои! Я сдаюсь, сдаюсь, дважды и трижды. Сдаюсь окончательно, бесповоротно, раз и навсегда. Всмотритесь наконец в меня, грешника! Какой же я, ко всем чертям, колдун? Я — Санчо Панса!

Дон Кихот. Что такое? Этот голос знаком мне. Ты не лжешь? Да это действительно ты, мой друг?

Санчо. Я, сеньор, я!

Дон Кихот. Почему же ты не подал мне условленного сигнала?

Санчо. Сударь, я троекратно подавал сигнал, но проклятый волшебник заложил вам уши. Я свистел, сударь!

Дон Кихот. Ведь ты был на волосок от гибели! Очень хорошо, что ты догадался сдаться. Ты поступил, Санчо, как мудрец, понимающий, что в отчаянном положении самый храбрый бережет себя для лучшего случая.

Санчо. Я сразу догадался, что нужно сдаться, лишь только вы начали тыкать мне в глаза вашим мечом, будь он проклят!

Дон Кихот. Ты прав. Но скажи мне, мой друг, читал ли ты где-нибудь о рыцаре, обладающем большей отвагой, нежели я?

Санчо. Нет, сударь, нигде не читал, потому что я не умею ни читать, ни писать.

Дон Кихот. Ну что ж, садись, и мы окончательно уговоримся обо всем, пока никого нет дома. Итак, ты принимаешь мое предложение стать моим оруженосцем и сопровождать меня во время странствований по свету?

Санчо. Принимаю, сеньор, так как надеюсь, что вы сдержите свое обещание сделать меня губернатором острова, который вы собираетесь завоевать.

Дон Кихот. Никогда не сомневайся в том, что сказано тебе рыцарем. Некоторых оруженосцев за их верную службу рыцари назначали властителями целых царств. И я надеюсь завоевать такое царство в самом скором времени. А так как самому мне оно не нужно, то я подарю его тебе. Ты станешь королем, Санчо.

Санчо. Гм... Об этом надо еще очень и очень подумать...

Дон Кихот. Что тебя смущает?

Санчо. Жена моя, Хуана Тереса.[12] Я опасаюсь, ваша милость, что королевская корона вряд ли придется ей по голове. Пусть уж она лучше будет простой губернаторшей, и дай бог, чтобы она справилась хоть с этим.

Дон Кихот. Положись во всем на волю провидения, Санчо, и сам никогда не унижайся и не желай себе меньшего, чем ты стоишь.

Санчо. Королем все-таки меня делать не надо, а стать губернатором я согласен.

Дон Кихот. Прекрасно. Теперь мы договорились обо всем, и самое время нам уехать тайно, пока никого нет.

Санчо. Это верно, сударь, а то ваша ключница... откровенно сказать вам, это такая женщина... я ее боюсь как огня!

Дон Кихот. Помоги мне надеть доспехи.

Санчо помогает Дон Кихоту надеть доспехи.

Посмотри, какой шлем я соорудил своими силами!

Санчо. Я немного опасаюсь, сударь, достаточно ли он прочен?

---

[12] In what seems to be a resolution to Cervantes's oversight, Bulgakov names Sancho's wife Juana Teresa. In the novel, Cervantes first names her Juana Gutiérrez and Mari Gutiérrez in volume 1, then Teresa Panza in volume 2.

Дон Кихот. Ах ты, маловер! Давай испытаем его. Надень его, я нанесу тебе самый сильный удар, какой только в состоянии нанести, и ты увидишь, чего он стоит.

Санчо. Слушаю, ваша милость. (*Надевает шлем.*)

Дон Кихот берет меч.

Стойте, сударь! Меня вдруг охватило дурное предчувствие. Давайте-ка лучше испытаем его, поставив на стол. (*Ставит шлем на стол.*)

Дон Кихот. Твоя трусость смешит меня. Смотри! (*Ударяет мечом по шлему и разбивает его вдребезги.*)

Санчо. Благодарю тебя, небо, за то, что в нем не было моей головы!

Дон Кихот. Ах!.. Ах!.. Это несчастье непоправимо! Без шлема мне нельзя тронуться в путь.

Санчо. Сеньор, лучше отправиться в путь совсем без шлема, чем в таком шлеме.

Дон Кихот. Что же нам делать? Ах, я безутешен... Ах, Санчо, гляди! (*Указывает на цирюльный таз.*)[13] Недаром говорится, что если перед кем-нибудь судьба закрывает одну дверь, то немедленно открывается какая-нибудь другая. О радость! Трусливый Фристон, убегая, забыл свой шлем!

[13] In the early modern era, barbers used a portable basin that had a wide rim with a semicircular opening designed to fit the neck, thus enabling the barber to shave the customer directly over the basin.

Санчо. Сеньор, это цирюльный таз, не будь я сыном своего отца!

Дон Кихот. Колдовство запорошило твои глаза. Смотри и убедись! (*Надевает таз на голову.*) Это шлем сарацинского короля Мамбрино.[14]

Санчо. Вылитый тазик для бритья.

Дон Кихот. Слепец!

Санчо. Как вам будет угодно ваша милость.

Дон Кихот. Ну вот все готово. Перед тобой нет более мирного идальго, Алонсо Кихано, прозванного Добрым! Я присваиваю себе новое имя — Дон Кихота Ламанчского![15]

Санчо. Слушаю, сударь!

Дон Кихот. А так как рыцарь, у которого нет дамы сердца, подобен дереву без листвы, то своей дамой я выбираю прекраснейшую из всех женщин

---

[14] King Mambrino, a Muslim, owned a golden helmet that purportedly made its wearer invulnerable. In Ludovico Ariosto's *Orlando Furioso* (1532), the knight Reinaldos de Montalbán wins the coveted helmet from Mambrino. Cervantes does not mention that Mambrino is from Saracinia. Bulgakov may have invented this word, basing it on *Saracen*.

[15] In Cervantes 1.1, Quixote spends eight days creating a new identity for himself. He does not, however, explicitly exchange the old identity for the new, as he does here. Another difference between the novel and the play is that in the novel Don Quixote is knighted by the innkeeper, a person who does not have the authority to do so. Don Quixote's knighthood therefore is questionable. Bulgakov omits the entire dubbing episode.

мира — принцессу Дульсинею из Тобосо. Ты знал ее, наверно, под именем Альдонсы Лоренсо.[16]

Санчо. Как не знать, сеньор! Но только вы напрасно называете ее принцессой, она простая крестьянка. Милейшая девушка, сеньор, а здоро́ва до того, что приятно взглянуть на нее. Любого рыцаря она способна одним взмахом выдернуть за бороду из грязи!

Дон Кихот. Перестань, несносный болтун! Пусть в твоих глазах Дульсинея не знатная дама, а крестьянка. Важно то, что для меня она чище, лучше и прекраснее всех принцесс. Ах, Санчо, я люблю ее, и этого достаточно, чтобы она затмила Диану![17] Я люблю ее, и это значит, что в моих глазах она бела, как снегопад, что ее лоб — Елисейские поля, а брови — небесные радуги.[18] О недалекий оруженосец! Поэт и рыцарь воспевает и любит не ту, что создана из плоти и крови, а ту, которую создала его неутомимая

---

[16] Although in Cervantes 1.1 the narrator identifies Aldonza Lorenzo as the true identity of Dulcinea del Toboso, Don Quixote himself does not admit to the connection until later (1.25). In contrast, Bulgakov's Don Quixote acknowledges from the start that Dulcinea and Aldonza are one and the same.

[17] Chivalric romances made abundant use of figures in Greek and Roman mythology.

[18] Focusing on the head, that is, the intellect, Bulgakov's Don Quixote reflects the platonic conventions of medieval courtly love poetry. Love in Bulgakov's time moved toward the platonic: Stalin-era films, plays, and books were expected to espouse modesty and chastity. In the analogous section of the novel (1.13), Don Quixote's presentation of Dulcinea is more erotic.

фантазия! Я люблю ее такой, какой она являлась мне в сновидениях! Я люблю, о Санчо, свой идеал! Понял ли, понял ли ты меня наконец? Или ты не знаешь слова "идеал"?

Санчо. Слова этого я не знаю, но я вас понял, сеньор. Теперь я вижу, что вы правы, а я осел. Да, вы правы, рыцарь печального образа![19]

Дон Кихот. Как? Как ты сказал?

Санчо. Рыцарь печального образа, сказал я, не гневайтесь на меня, сударь.

Дон Кихот. Почему ты произнес такие слова?

Санчо. Я глядел на вас сейчас при свете луны,[20] и у вас было такое скорбное лицо, какого мне не приходилось видеть. Быть может, вы утомились в боях, или произошло это оттого, что у вас не хватает нескольких зубов справа и спереди. Кто выбил их вам, сеньор?

---

[19] Cervantes 1.19. In Spanish,"El caballero de la Triste Figura" ("knight of the sad face"). In the novel, Sancho gives Don Quixote this moniker when, after Don Quixote has lost a number of teeth in the battle with the sheep and their shepherds, his face has become sunken and sallow (1.18); in the play, Don Quixote appears as such from the start.

[20] The moon is an important symbol in Bulgakov's work as a whole and in the play in particular. Note that the word for "moon" (луна, *luna*) is the same in both Russian and Spanish. It is the root for the English *lunatic* and the Spanish *lunático*, and madness is a major theme in both the play and Мастер и Маргарита.

Дон Кихот. Это несущественно! Интересно то, что внезапно налетевшая мудрость вложила в твои уста эти слова. И знай, что с этого мгновения я так и буду называть себя, а на щите моем я велю изобразить печальную фигуру.

Санчо. Зачем, сеньор, вам тратить на это деньги? Стоит вам открыть лицо — и всякий сразу смекнет, кто стоит перед ним.

Дон Кихот. Э! Под твоей довольно туповатой наружностью скрывается колкий человек! Ну что же, пусть я буду рыцарем Печального Образа — я с гордостью принимаю это наименование, — но этот печальный рыцарь рожден для того, чтобы наш бедственный железный век превратить в век златой![21] Я тот, кому суждены опасности и беды, но также и

---

[21] In the context of Stalin's Russia, this speech can be read as a veiled criticism of the rapid industrialization and collectivization the country was undergoing. Russia struggled to recover from the economic devastation of the Civil War (1917–21) with the aid of the New Economic Policy (NEP), which allowed for some market flexibility in the newly established socialist system. However, in the late 1920s Stalin replaced NEP with a system of centrally controlled five-year plans, whose success depended on drastically lowering the consumption of ordinary Soviet citizens and on the ruthless extraction of capital from the kulaks (relatively affluent peasants who resisted collectivization). The plans produced economic growth but at the cost of millions of lives and the free labor of prisoners and young Communist activists. For many Soviet citizens, then, the iron age of socialist reconstruction signified a complete break with the humanistic ideals of a previous golden time that valued the individual above all else.

великие подвиги! Идем же вперед, Санчо, и воскресим прославленных рыцарей Круглого Стола! Летим по свету, чтобы мстить за обиды, нанесенные свирепыми и сильными — беспомощным и слабым, чтобы биться за поруганную честь, чтобы вернуть миру то, что он безвозвратно потерял, — справедливость!

Санчо. Ах, сеньор рыцарь, хорошо, кабы это все сбылось! А то не раз мне приходилось слышать, что люди отправляются стричь овец, а возвращаются сами остриженными.[22]

Дон Кихот. Нет, не смущай мою душу своими пословицами... Я не хочу, чтобы меня терзали сомнения! Поспешим, Санчо, пока не вернулись домашние.

Выходят во двор.

Сейчас ты увидишь моего коня, он ничем не хуже Буцефала, на котором ездил Александр Македонский.[23] (*Открывает дверь конюшни.*) Я назвал его Росинантом.[24]

[22] The Spanish proverb "Ir por lana y salir trasquilado" ("Go for wool and come back shorn") appears four times in Cervantes's novel (1.7, 2.14, 2.43, 2.67). It applies to people who seek more than they have and end up with less or who expect a benefit and suffer a loss or injury instead.

[23] Alexander the Great (356–323 BC) conquered and briefly united under Macedonian rule much of the world then known to the Greeks. Bucephalus was the most famous horse of antiquity and Alexander's companion through most of his military campaigns.

[24] In Spanish, *rocín* ("nag") and *ante* ("foremost").

Санчо (*осмотрев Росинанта*). Кто был этот Македонский, сударь?

Дон Кихот. Я расскажу тебе о нем дорогой. Поспешим. Но позволь, на чем же поедешь ты?

Санчо. На своем ослике, сударь.

Дон Кихот. Э... Мне не приходилось читать, чтобы оруженосцы ездили на ослах...

Санчо. Прекрасный крепкий ослик, сударь...

Дон Кихот. Ну что же поделаешь, едем! Прощай, мое родное и мирное селение, прощай! Вперед, Санчо, луна освещает наш путь, и к утру мы будем далеко-далеко. Вперед!

Санчо. Вперед! Но!..

Уезжают.

КАРТИНА ВТОРАЯ

Летнее утро. Перекресток дорог. С одной стороны лес, с другой — поле. Видно крыло ветряной мельницы. Выезжают Дон Кихот и Санчо и останавливаются.

Дон Кихот. Вот мы и достигли перекрестка, Санчо. Я уверен, что здесь полными пригоршнями мы будем черпать из озера приключений. (*Смотрит вдаль.*)

Санчо слезает с осла и привязывает его в стороне от дороги.

Судьба благосклонна к нам. Гляди, гляди туда, Санчо!

Санчо. Я ничего не вижу, сеньор.

Дон Кихот. Неужели ты ослеп? Почему ты не поражаешься? Перед нами строй гигантов с длиннейшими костлявыми руками!

Санчо. Помилуйте, сеньор, это ветряные мельницы!

Дон Кихот. Как мало смыслишь ты в рыцарских приключениях. Это злые волшебники-великаны, и я немедленно вступлю с ними в бой! Я истреблю эту злую породу!

Мельницы начинают двигать крыльями.

Вы не испугаете меня, хотя бы рук у вас было больше, чем у великана Бриарея! Не бегите, мерзкие созданья! Против вас только один рыцарь, но он один стоит вас всех!

Санчо. Опомнитесь, сударь, что вы собираетесь делать?

Дон Кихот. А, страх охватил тебя! Ну что же, оставайся здесь под деревьями и читай молитвы! Вперед, во имя прекрасной и жестокой покорительницы сердца Дульсинеи! (*Пришпоривает Росинанта и уезжает.*)

Санчо. Сеньор, остановитесь! Сеньор, куда вы? (*Становится на колени.*) Господи, господи, что же это делает мой господин? Силы небесные, он на крыло бросился с копьем! Сеньор!! Стойте! Так и есть, потащило! Потащило!.. Господи, помилуй нас, грешных!

За сценой тяжелый удар. На сцену выкатывается цирюльный таз, затем падают обломки копья, а затем обрушивается Дон Кихот и остается лежать неподвижен.

Так я и знал!.. Царство ему небесное! Как быстро закончились наши приключения! Ах, подумать только, вчера вечером мы выехали с ним живые и здоровые, полные надежд, и не успел я дослушать до конца рассказ про изумительную лошадь Александра Македонского, как мой почтенный господин с перебитыми ребрами перелетел в другой мир! Эх, эх, эх!.. (*Снимает с осла бурдюк, садится рядом с Дон Кихотом, пьет вино.*) Как же я повезу его домой? Придется положить его поперек седла... А поперек какого седла? (*Смотрит вдаль.*) Бедная лошадь лежит неподвижно, как куль с ячменем. Придется класть его на осла. Бедный друг мой, ты никогда еще не носил такой печальной ноши.

Дон Кихот простонал.

Кто стонет здесь? Мой господин стонать не может, он мертв. Уж не сам ли я простонал от горя? (*Пьет вино.*)

Дон Кихот (*слабо*). Санчо...

Санчо. Что слышу я? Вы живы, сеньор?

Дон Кихот. Раз я подаю голос, значит, я жив.

Санчо. Благодарение небу, сеньор! А я уже собирался взвалить вас на своего серого, чтобы везти вас в деревню и там похоронить с почестями, которых вы заслуживаете. И при мысли о том, что мне скажет ключница, я отчаянно страдал, сеньор! Хлебните!.. Эх, сударь, сударь, ведь я же вас предупреждал, что это мельницы!

Дон Кихот. Никогда не рассуждай о том, чего ты не понимаешь, Санчо, и знай, что и впереди нас ждут постоянные чародейства и волшебные изменения. Проклятый мудрец, все тот же ненавистный Фристон, лишь только я вонзил свое копье в руку первого из великанов, немедленно превратил их всех в мельницы, чтобы отнять у меня сладость победы. Фристон, Фристон! Доколе меня будет преследовать твоя ненависть и зависть?.. Приведи ко мне моего коня.

Санчо. Даже сам Фристон, сеньор, не в состоянии это сделать. Бедное животное лежит неподвижно. Самое лучшее — дать коню отлежаться, и, если провидению будет угодно, он поднимется сам, если же нет — наша забота о нем будет заключаться только в одном: мы снимем с него его старую шкуру и продадим ее на первом же базаре. Эх, сударь!

Дон Кихот. Подай мне мое копье.

Санчо. Не много проку теперь от этого копья, ваша милость. (*Подает Дон Кихоту обломки копья.*)

Дон Кихот. Ах, это серьезная утрата! Что может сделать рыцарь без копья? Впрочем, не будем тужить. Ведь ты читал, конечно...

Санчо. Ах, сударь, ведь я же говорил вам уже!..

Дон Кихот. Ах да, ведь ты не мог читать.

Санчо. Не мог, сударь, не мог.

Дон Кихот. Ну, так я тебе скажу, что храбрый рыцарь Дон Диего Перес де Варгас,[25] лишившись в бою оружия, отломил от дуба громадный сук и в тот же день перебил им столько мавров, что тела их лежали, как дрова на черном дворе.

Санчо. Как звали его, сударь?

Дон Кихот. Дон Диего Перес де Варгас. Принеси мне сук потяжелее, Санчо.

Санчо. Слушаю, сеньор. (*Уходит и возвращается с громадным суком, надевает на него наконечник копья.*) Вот вам новое копье. Желаю вам наколотить мавров

---

[25] A historical thirteenth-century knight from Toledo nicknamed Machuca ("bruiser").

не меньше, чем наколотил... Эх, выскользнуло из памяти, а красивое имя.

Дон Кихот. Дон Диего Перес де Варгас. Он не один, Санчо, бил мавров. Доблестный Родриго Нарваэсский, алькад крепости Антекера, взял в плен сеньора мавра Абиндараэса как раз в тот момент, когда тот испускал свой страшный боевой клич: "Лелилиес!"[26]

Санчо. Вас совсем перекосило набок, сударь.

Дон Кихот. Да, мой друг, страшнейшая боль терзает меня, и я не жалуюсь на нее лишь потому, что рыцарям запрещено это делать.

Санчо. Если вам запрещено, ничего не поделаешь, молчите. Но про себя я скажу, сударь, что я буду стонать и жаловаться, если со мной случится что-нибудь вроде того, что с вами. Или, быть может, запрещение жаловаться касается и оруженосцев?

Дон Кихот. Нет, в уставе ордена об оруженосцах нет ни слова по этому поводу.

Санчо. Очень рад этому.

[26] Rodrígo de Narváez was a fifteenth-century nobleman and mayor of the town of Antequera. He is the Christian protagonist of *Abencerraje y la hermosa Jarifa* (1561; "The Abencerraje and the Beautiful Jarifa"). Abindarráez is the novel's Muslim protagonist. "Lelilíes" is the Spanish word for Muslim war cries.

Дон Кихот. Постой, постой! Я вижу пыль на дороге. Да, это место незаменимо для приключений! Но, Санчо, я должен тебя предупредить, что, сколько бы ни увлекала тебя твоя горячность, ты не должен браться за меч, в какой бы опасности я ни находился, разве что на меня нападут люди твоего звания.

Санчо. Вам не придется повторять два раза этот приказ, сударь.

Дон Кихот. Смотри туда! Я был прав. Ты видишь, идут две черные фигуры в масках, а там вдалеке за ними — карета. Все понятно: эти двое — волшебники, а в карете — принцесса, которую они похищают!

Санчо. Я советую вам немного одуматься, сеньор! Эти двое в черном — монахи, за ними идут их слуги, и никаких волшебников нет!

Дон Кихот. Ты близорук или вовсе слеп!

Санчо. Сударь, это дельце будет похуже, чем с ветряными мельницами!

Дон Кихот. Не мешай мне! Твое дело — следить за боем, а затем овладеть богатейшей добычей, которая нам достанется.

Показываются двое монахов.

Стойте, черные дьяволы!

Санчо прячется за дерево.

Стойте! Я требую, чтобы вы немедленно вернули свободу этой даме в карете! Вы обманом завлекли несчастную в плен!

Первый монах. Что такое? Мы ничего не понимаем, сударь! Какая дама? Мы — мирные бенедиктинцы, следуем своей дорогой и к этой карете не имеем никакого отношения... Она и повернула-то совсем на другую дорогу.

Дон Кихот. Я не поверю вашим обманным словам!

Первый монах. Сударь, вы в каком-то странном заблуждении...

Дон Кихот. Молчать!

Санчо (за деревом). Молчать!

Дон Кихот. Сейчас вы испробуете, коварные, силу моего меча! (*Выхватывает меч.*)

Первый монах. Помогите! Слуги! На помощь! Здесь разбойники! (*Убегает.*)

Второй монах. На помощь!

Дон Кихот (*убегая вслед за Первым монахом*). Остановись, гнусное отродье! Ты мой, ты побежден!

Санчо (*пронзительно свистит, выскакивает из-за дерева, бросается ко Второму монаху*). Лелилиес! Ты побежден, ты мой!

Второй монах (*падая на колени*). О небо, защити меня!

Санчо. Снимай одёжу, проклятый Перес де Варгас! (*Срывает с монаха шляпу и маску.*)

Второй монах. Берите все, но оставьте жизнь! (*Отдает одежду Санчо.*)

В это время вбегают двое слуг.

Защитите меня! (*Убегает.*)

Первый слуга. Ты что же это делаешь, окаянный разбойник, на большой дороге?!

Второй слуга. Грабитель!

Санчо. Ну-ну-ну, отойдите от меня, милые люди, это вас не касается. Моя добыча, и дело с концом! Мы победили волшебников, а не вы!

Второй слуга. Ах ты, наглый бродяга!

Первый слуга. Бей его!

Слуги бросаются на Санчо с палками.

Санчо. Что вы, взбесились, что ли? Сеньор, на помощь! Отнимают добычу у вашего оруженосца!

Первый слуга. Ах ты, мошенник!

Второй слуга. Вот тебе! (*Вцепляется в бороду Санчо.*)

Слуги нещадно бьют Санчо.

Санчо. Сеньор!.. Сеньор!.. Сеньор!.. Лелилиес!.. (*Падает и остается неподвижен.*)

Второй слуга. Будешь знать, как раздевать прохожих!

Слуги убегают с одеждой монаха.

Дон Кихот (*вбегает*). Убежал презренный, как заяц в поле!.. Что с тобой? Боже, да он мертв!! Что же мне теперь делать?..

Санчо. Ох...

Дон Кихот. Ты жив?!

Санчо. Если я подаю голос — чтоб меня черти взяли! — стало быть, я жив... И если я еще раз...

Дон Кихот. Ах, проклятая память! Если бы я не забыл перед отъездом приготовить склянку Фьерабрасова бальзама, нам с тобой не были бы страшны никакие раны!

Санчо. Что это за бальзам, сударь?

Дон Кихот. Это чудодейственное лекарство, Санчо. Если ты когда-нибудь увидишь, что меня в бою разрубили пополам — а это нередко случается со странствующими рыцарями, — не теряйся. Возьми обе половинки, сложи их, но только поаккуратнее, конечно, и дай мне глотка два этого бальзама. Ты увидишь, что я мгновенно поднимусь на ноги и стану свеж и здоров, как яблоко. Вот какое это лекарство, Санчо.

Санчо. Сударь, мне не нужно губернаторства на острове, которое вы мне великодушно обещали. Снабдите меня рецептом этого бальзама.

Дон Кихот. Не беспокойся, мой друг, я сообщу тебе еще более удивительные тайны и облагодетельствую тебя на всю жизнь.

Санчо. В таком случае, сеньор, я счастлив, что поехал с вами... и даже боль моя как будто стала уменьшаться... (*Разворачивает вьюк, достает провизию.*) Следует подкрепиться, сударь. Впрочем, вы не станете есть моей простой пищи.

Дон Кихот. У тебя неверное представление о рыцарях, мой друг. Рыцари ели хорошо только на торжественных пирах, устраиваемых в их честь, а в обычное время, то есть во время странствований, они питались чем попало, а большей частью, увы, цветами и мечтами.[27]

Санчо. Цветов у меня нет, сударь, есть хлеб, чеснок, сыр и желуди, а мечтание у меня теперь только одно — овладеть рецептом вашего бальзама. Кушайте, сударь.

Дон Кихот. Садись и ты, что же ты стоишь, мой друг? О чем ты задумался?

Санчо. Я вот думаю о том, как вы, рыцарь, едите мою простую пищу?

Дон Кихот. А я думаю о другом. Ты вот сказал: мою пищу. Я думаю о том веке, когда не было этих слов: мое и твое. Когда люди, мирно сидя, вот как мы

[27] Don Quixote's comment is especially poignant when we consider his character an example of the struggling Soviet artist. Many writers who fell out of favor during Stalin's regime were reduced to poverty. Much like the knights in Don Quixote's interpretation, they subsisted on the most meager of rations and their dreams of escape.

сейчас сидим с тобой на зеленой траве, щедро делились друг с другом тем, что им послала благостная, ни в чем не отказывающая природа. Да и что людям, пасшим свои стада, было прятать друг от друга? Прозрачные ключи давали им воду, а деревья — плоды. Не было золота, которое породило ложь, обман, злобу и корыстолюбие, и хоть его и не было — этот век, Санчо, назывался золотым веком, и вот мечтание странствующего рыцаря, как я уже говорил тебе, заключается в том, чтобы возродить этот сверкающий век![28] Ах, Санчо, если бы на мою долю не выпало тревожное счастье стать рыцарем, я хотел бы быть пастухом! Я назвался бы Кихотисом, а ты — Пансино, и мы стали бы бродить по горам и лугам, то распевая романсы, то вздыхая от полноты души. Днем нас спасала бы от жгучего солнца буйная листва дубов, а ночью нам светили бы мирные звезды. Ах, неужели ты не понимаешь, что только в такой жизни человек может найти настоящее счастье, что это его наилучший удел?

Санчо. Вы — ученый человек, сеньор, и знаете множество интересного. Так что если вы начнете

[28] This brief speech corresponds to a much lengthier one in Cervantes 1.11, which speaks to the classical notion of the four ages of man (golden, silver, bronze, and iron). The speech also presages Quixote's intention to take up the pastoral life, late in the second book, after his defeat by Sansón Carrasco (2.67).

рассказывать, вас можно слушать развесив уши целыми часами. Но самое интересное — это бальзам. Быть может, все-таки вы мне сообщите рецепт сейчас? А то потом, чего доброго, во время приключений и забудется...

Дон Кихот. А я-то полагал, что ты задумался о золотом веке. Потерпи: лишь только мы приедем куда-нибудь под кров, я приготовлю бальзам и открою тебе его секрет.

Вдали послышались мужские голоса, кто-то насвистывает песенку.

Кто там такой?

Санчо (*всматриваясь*). Это компания погонщиков лошадей, сеньор, из Янгуэсского округа. Лихие ребята, сударь, эти янгуэсы, и дружные такие! Я полагаю, что они с ярмарки возвращаются.

Вдали послышался хохот.

Дон Кихот. Что их рассмешило?

Санчо. Да один из них ударил вашего Росинанта. Они смеются над ним, сеньор.

Дон Кихот. Что ты сказал? Наглец осмелился затронуть рыцарскую лошадь? Клянусь, что я не успокоюсь до тех пор, пока мы не проучим всю эту компанию негодяев!

Санчо. Помилуйте, сударь, как это мы их проучим, когда их двадцать человек по крайней мере, а нас только двое, или, вернее, полтора человека!

Дон Кихот. Ты забыл, что я один стою больше, чем целая сотня врагов!

Входят трое погонщиков.

Смелее, Санчо, потребуй их к ответу!

Санчо (*Первому погонщику*). Ты зачем ударил чужую лошадь?

Первый погонщик. Какую такую лошадь?

Санчо. Не строй из себя дурака!

Второй погонщик. Ах эту! Что лежит кверху ногами? А мы думали, что это не лошадь, а скелет.

Входит Четвертый погонщик.

Дон Кихот. Ты, каналья, смеешь смеяться над лошадью славнейшего в мире рыцаря?

Санчо. Да, каналья, я тебя требую к ответу, ты смеешь?

Второй погонщик. Да, смею.

Санчо. Смеешь?

Погонщики. Смеем!

Входит Пятый погонщик.

Санчо. Так нá же тебе! (*Дает в ухо Второму погонщику.*)

Второй погонщик. А вот тебе сдачи! (*Дает в ухо Санчо.*)

Санчо. На помощь, сеньор!

Дон Кихот (*ударив плашмя копьем Третьего погонщика*). Защищайся, презренный сброд!

Третий погонщик. На помощь, ребята!

Первый погонщик. На помощь, ребята! Наших янгуэсов бьют!

Вбегают Шестой и Седьмой погонщики.

Четвертый погонщик (*ударив Санчо*). Сюда, братцы! Наших янгуэсов бьют!

Пятый погонщик (*ударив Дон Кихота*). Не выдавай, ребята, наших!

Шестой погонщик (*бросается на Дон Кихота, отнимает у него копье*). Не робей, ребята.

Седьмой погонщик (*ударив Санчо*). Сюда, ребята! Наших бьют!

Вбегает Восьмой погонщик.

Погонщики (*набрасываясь на Дон Кихота, валят его на землю*). Не выдавай, ребята! (*Бьют Санчо.*)

Санчо (*пытаясь защищаться*). На помощь, сеньор, нас бьют!!

Четвертый погонщик. Защищайся, ребята, на нас напали!

Погонщики бьют Санчо и Дон Кихота смертным боем. Вбегают Девятый, Десятый и Одиннадцатый погонщики, набрасываются на Санчо и Дон Кихота.

Санчо. Караул! Говорил я... Говорил я... Сеньор!!

Дон Кихот (*хрипя*). Презренные!.. Санчо, на помощь!..

Санчо. Абиндараэс... (*Затихает.*)

Двенадцатый погонщик (*вбегает*). Стойте, черти, стойте! Обрадовались! В ответ за них попадем! Гляди, они не дышат!

Первый погонщик. Стой, черти, стой!

Второй погонщик. Довольно, черти, стой!

Погонщики. Стой, черти, стой! Стой, стой, стой!..

Первый погонщик. Довольно, ребята! Ну их к дьяволу, этих забияк!

Второй и Третий погонщики. Мы так испугались!..

Второй погонщик. Этот меня по уху раз!..

Первый погонщик. Да ну их к дьяволу, влетит из-за них! Айда отсюда, ребята!

Погонщики. Айда отсюда.

Все погонщики уходят. На траве остаются неподвижные Дон Кихот и Санчо. Грустный ослик стоит возле них.

Конец первого действия.

ДЕЙСТВИЕ ВТОРОЕ

КАРТИНА ТРЕТЬЯ

Летний вечер. Постоялый двор Паломека Левши.[29] *Колодезь, ворота на заднем плане, раскрытый сарай с дырявой крышей, два флигеля. Из окон одного из них слышится хохот, звон стаканов — там ужинает веселая компания постояльцев. Мариторнес развешивает белье на веревке.*

Мариторнес (*напевает*).

Вот лежит пастух безгласный.
На груди широкой кровь.
Отчего погиб несчастный?
Он зарезан за любовь...

Погонщик мулов. Здорово, красотка!

---

[29] Левша, literally "lefty," can also mean "master" or "someone skilled at what he does." The name echoes the title of Nikolai Leskov's 1881 story "Сказ о тульском косом Левше и о стальной блохе," which is about a Russian craftsman who bests his English counterpart in a competition.

Мариторнес. Ах! Как не стыдно так пугать людей? Здравствуйте!

Погонщик мулов. Здравствуй, Мариторнес! А я ведь тебя давненько не видал и соскучился по тебе. Надо сказать, что ты очень похорошела за это время!

Мариторнес. Ах, перестаньте шутить!

Погонщик мулов. Я не шучу, драгоценная Мариторнес. Пойди-ка сюда ко мне поближе, я тебе хочу что-то шепнуть.

Мариторнес. Как вам не стыдно!

Погонщик мулов. Вот тебе раз! Да откуда ты знаешь, что́ я хочу тебе шепнуть?

Мариторнес. Нам известно, о чем шепчут на ухо... (*Напевает.*) “Вот лежит пастух безгласный...”

Погонщик мулов. Ну, слушай... сегодня я намерен ночевать у вас... так вот, когда все угомонятся... ты меня навести...

Мариторнес. Ишь, что выдумал! Да ни за что на свете! А где же тебя поместит хозяин?

Погонщик мулов. Я попрошусь в сарай.

Паломек (*во флигеле*). Мариторнес! Мариторнес!

Мариторнес. Отойди от меня! Слышишь, хозяин зовет!

Паломек (*выглянув в окно*). Мариторнес! Где эта дрянная девица?

Мариторнес. Что это вы так раскричались? Я здесь, где же мне еще быть?

Паломек. Ты что там делаешь?

Мариторнес. А что же мне делать? Видите, белье вешаю.

Паломек. Знаем мы это белье! С тебя глаз нельзя спускать.

Погонщик мулов (*выходя из-за белья*). Здорово, хозяин! Здравствуйте, сеньор Паломек Левша!

Паломек. Ах вот оно какое белье! Что это за необыкновенная девица! Скажите на милость! Чуть только отвернешься — начинаются шашни!

Погонщик мулов. Нет, хозяин, вы напрасно браните ее, она хорошая девушка. Я только что вошел во двор и не успел ей сказать и трех слов...

Паломек. Разные бывают слова. Иные три слова хуже, чем целая длинная речь. Эта красотка всем известна.

Мариторнес. Мало того, что всякие семейные несчастья вынудили меня служить на постоялом дворе за гроши...

Паломек. Ну-ну-ну, довольно, перестань хныкать, бездельница!

Мариторнес скрывается.

Ты ко мне?

Погонщик мулов. Да, хочу у вас переночевать.

Паломек. Все занято, нет ни одной постели... разве что в сарай... В сарай желаешь?

Погонщик мулов. Это, стало быть, укрываться небом со звездами? Ведь крыша-то у вас дырявая?

Паломек. Ах, простите, почтеннейший сеньор! Ежели бы я знал, что вы пожалуете к нам, я бы приготовил вам дворец под золотой крышей и с шелковыми одеялами. Не нравится — ступай, ночуй в поле. Я ведь тебя не приглашал, говорю, что все занято.

Погонщик мулов. Ну ладно, ладно, согласен в сарай.

Паломек. Нá попону! (*Выбрасывает в окно попону.*) Подстели, заснешь, как на перине, по-королевски, еще все завидовать будут.

Погонщик мулов берет попону и, проходя мимо Мариторнес, делает какие-то таинственные знаки.

Мариторнес (*тихо*). Что вы, что вы!.. (*Напевает.*) "Отчего же на нем кровь? Нож ему вонзили в сердце, и погиб он за любовь..."

Эрнандес (*в окне флигеля*). Эй, хозяин! Дайте-ка нам еще винца!

Паломек. Сию минуту, сеньоры! (*Пробегает во флигель с бурдюком, потом возвращается к себе.*)

Из флигеля доносится хохот, зазвенели струны.

Эрнандес (*во флигеле поет*). “Ах, маркиз мой Мантуанский, Мантуанский, Мантуанский, дядя мой и господин!..”

В ворота входит Санчо, согнувшись в три погибели, и ведет в поводу своего осла. На осле — полуживой Дон Кихот. Сзади идет хромающий Росинант, нагруженный измятыми доспехами и самодельным копьем. Голова Санчо обвязана тряпкой, под глазом синяк, половина бороды выдрана.

Санчо. Благодарение небесам, добрались до постоялого двора! Ох!.. (*Садится на край колодца.*) Эй, девушка... девушка!.. Подойди-ка сюда!

Мариторнес. Вот так так! Таких у нас еще не бывало!

Санчо (*Дон Кихоту*). Очнитесь, сеньор, приехали на постоялый двор!

Дон Кихот. Что?

Санчо. Держите себя бодрее, сударь, а то вы похожи на мешок с навозом. Мы прибыли на постоялый двор.

Дон Кихот. Что говоришь ты, Санчо? Мы прибыли в замок? Подожди, сейчас выйдет карлик, протрубит, подъемный мост спустят, и мы войдем...

Санчо. Какие там мосты и карлики, сеньор! Очнитесь!

Послышался звук рога Свинопаса.

Дон Кихот. Маловерный оруженосец, ты слышишь трубные звуки? Это нас встречают. (*Кряхтя, слезает с осла.*)

Мариторнес. Вот потеха-то!

Дон Кихот (*Мариторнес*). О прекрасная сеньора! Позвольте мне представиться вам. Я — странствующий рыцарь Дон Кихот Ламанчский, которого молва прозвала рыцарем Печального Образа. Я — тот рыцарь, подвиги коего затмили подвиги Пылающего Меча и Рейнальдоса де Монтальбана, похитившего золотой идол Магомета! Я — ваш покорный слуга!

Мариторнес. Ах, чувствительно вам благодарна, кавальеро![30] (*Санчо.*) Он так сладко говорит, так хорошо, но до того чудно́, до того чудно́, что ничего не поймешь!

Погонщик мулов (*выглядывая из сарая*). Это что такое? Кажется, эта облезлая крыса подъезжает к Мариторнес?

Мариторнес (*Санчо*). Он что же, грек, что ли?

---

[30] In modern Spanish, *caballero* means "gentleman," but in the Middle Ages it meant "knight" or "horseman."

Санчо. Грек, грек, только устрой нам, девушка, переночевать.

Мариторнес. Хозяин! Хозяин!

Паломек (*выглядывая из окна*). Чего тебе надо?

Мариторнес. Принимайте постояльцев.

Паломек (*вытаращив глаза, глядит на Дон Кихота, потом выходит*). Чем могу служить?

Дон Кихот. Сеньор кастелян,[31] вы видите перед собой рыцаря, принадлежащего к ордену странствующих, и его оруженосца.

Паломек. Как вы говорите?.. Ордена?!

Дон Кихот. Мы были бы вам крайне признательны, если бы вы приютили нас в вашем замке.

Паломек. Сеньор кавальеро, всем, за исключением комнаты и постели — нет ни одной свободной, — могу служить вам.

Дон Кихот. Мы удовольствуемся малым, ибо битва — отдых для рыцаря, оружие — его украшение, а ложе его — твердые скалы.

Погонщик мулов. Ишь как размазывает, черт бы его побрал!

Паломек. Ну, если так, сударь, то лучшего места, чем у меня в сарае, вам не найти!

[31] A castellan is a castle warden.

Погонщик мулов. Кой черт, хозяин, ведь вы же мне отдали сарай.

Паломек. Там и для троих достаточно места. (*Дон Кихоту*.) А где это вас так отделали, сударь?

Санчо. Это он со скалы упал.

Мариторнес. С какой же скалы? Тут у нас и скал-то нет.

Санчо. Раз я говорю, что упал со скалы, значит, есть где-то скала.

Паломек (*Санчо*). А тебя, что ли, тоже угораздило сверзиться со скалы?

Санчо. Ох, и меня... То есть я не падал, а как увидел, что он упал, сейчас же почувствовал, что и сам весь разбит.

Мариторнес. Ах, это бывает! Я иногда вижу во сне, что падаю, и просыпаюсь совсем, совсем разбитая!

Паломек. Знаем мы, что ты видишь во сне, можешь не рассказывать! Эй!

Вбегает Работник.

Бери лошадь и осла, ставь в конюшню.

Дон Кихот. Я покорнейше прошу вас, сеньор кастелян, позаботиться хорошенько об этой лошади, потому что это лучшая верховая лошадь, какая когда-нибудь существовала на свете!

Погонщик мулов. Вот эта? (*Делает Паломеку знаки, означающие, что Дон Кихот не в своем уме.*)

Работник уводит осла и Росинанта.

Санчо (*Дон Кихоту*). Вы бы рассказали им, сеньор, про Македонского, а то они не верят вам. Пойдемте-ка в сарай. (*Уводит Дон Кихота в сарай.*)

Все расходятся со двора.

Как вы полагаете, сеньор, через сколько времени мы с вами будем в состоянии шевелить ногами, я уже не говорю — ходить?

Дон Кихот. Признаю, что во всем том, что произошло, безусловно виноват я. Мне ни в коем случае не следовало поднимать меч против людей, не принадлежащих к рыцарскому званию. Если когда-нибудь еще на нас нападет шайка вроде сегодняшней, мы поступим так: я даже не притронусь к мечу, ты же вынимай свой и руби их безжалостно. Если же за них заступятся рыцари, тогда только я вступлю в дело и уж сумею защитить тебя. Хороший план?

Санчо. Очень хороший, сеньор, пусть меня убьет громом! Вот что, сударь: я — человек миролюбивый, тихий, кроткий, спокойный, добродушный и покладистый, это — во-первых. Во-вторых, у меня нет меча, чему я очень рад, и в-третьих, я не выну его ни против человека простого звания, ни против дворянина, ни против крестьянина, ни против рыцаря, ни против козопаса, свинопаса, черта или дьявола!

Дон Кихот. Как жаль, что у меня от боли захватывает дыхание, а то я возразил бы тебе как следует. Одно могу лишь сказать — что с таким миролюбием, как твое, тебе следует стать пастухом Пансино, а управлять островом тебе нельзя. Ведь ты будешь иметь дело с врагами, а для этого требуется мужество. Несчастный! Пойми, что бури, подобные сегодняшней, неразрывно связаны с нашим званием, и без них оно бы потеряло всякую прелесть.

Санчо. Вы мне скажите только одно, сеньор: урожаи, вроде того, что мы собрали сегодня, беспрерывно будут следовать один за другим, или между ними будут все-таки какие-нибудь промежутки? А то, чего доброго, собрав два из них, мы к третьему можем оказаться и вовсе неспособными?

Дон Кихот. Забудь о горести, постигшей нас, Санчо. Нет воспоминания, которое устояло бы против времени, нет и боли, которую не исцелила бы смерть. Сейчас мы приступим к приготовлению Фьерабрасова бальзама.

Санчо (*оживившись*). Что требуется для этого, сударь, скажите? Эй, девушка, девушка!

Мариторнес. Чего вам?

Санчо. Вот что, голубушка: мы сейчас бальзам будем приготовлять...

Мариторнес. Какой бальзам?

Санчо. Это, душенька, бальзам волшебный! Одного, понимаешь ли, в бою разрубили пополам... ох!... дали ему хлебнуть, и он пошел рубить мавров!..

Мариторнес. Дайте мне попробовать хоть немножечко, у меня такая тоска на сердце, как будто его кошка скребет когтями!

Санчо. Так и быть, дадим. (*Дон Кихоту.*) Так чего, сударь, требуется?

Дон Кихот. Возьмите большую кастрюлю...

Санчо (*Мариторнес*). Слышишь, кастрюлю?

Мариторнес. Кастрюлю.

Дон Кихот. Влейте в нее пять бутылок сладкого красного вина.

Санчо (*Мариторнес*). Понимаешь?

Мариторнес. Понимаю.

Дон Кихот. Положите туда пригоршню тертого чесноку.

Санчо (*Мариторнес*). Запомнила — пригоршню чесноку?

Погонщик мулов (*входит*). Это что такое будет?

Мариторнес. Они бальзам знают... бальзам будут приготовлять. Такой бальзам... Одного, понимаешь, разрубили пополам...

Погонщик мулов. Ага, ага!

Дон Кихот. Соли ложек четыре или пять, больших.

Санчо (*Мариторнес*). Ты послушай!

Погонщик мулов. Я запомню. Соли пять ложек. Это правильно.

Мариторнес (*загибая пальцы*). Пять.

Дон Кихот. Щепотку красного перцу... желудей тертых горсть, уксусу, три бутылки лампадного масла и маленькую ложечку купоросного масла.

Погонщик мулов. Все правильно. Я этот бальзам знаю.

Дон Кихот. Все хорошенько размешать и подогреть на огне.

Мариторнес. Поняла, сейчас сделаю.

Погонщик мулов. Я тебе помогу. Это хороший бальзам, он даже мулам помогает, в особенности от чесотки.

Мариторнес, Погонщик мулов и Санчо уходят в кухню.

Паломек (*появляется в сарае*). Почтенный сеньор, моя служанка сказала мне, что вы владеете секретом всеисцеляющего бальзама. Я счастлив, сеньор, что судьба привела вас ко мне. Все, что требуется, уже выдано мною служанке. Я надеюсь, что и мне вы дадите испробовать этого лекарства? В последнее время меня очень мучает поясница. А я, со своей стороны, готов вам служить наилучшим образом.

Дон Кихот. Я с удовольствием исполню вашу просьбу, сеньор кастелян.

Паломек. Как ножом режет поясницу!

Работник (*с кружечкой*). Сударь.

Паломек. Тебе чего надо?

Работник. Бальзаму хочу попросить... Громаднейший ячмень на глазу.

Паломек. Ну-ну-ну, нечего, не помрешь ты от этого!

Дон Кихот. Не гоните его, сеньор кастелян, надо пожалеть и его. Я охотно дам ему этого бальзама.

Паломек. Ну, если вы так великодушны, сеньор...

Появляются Мариторнес с кастрюлей в руках, Санчо, Погонщик мулов и Слуга дона Мартинеса, все с кружечками.

Мариторнес. Готово, сударь.

Паломек (*Слуге Мартинеса*). А тебе что?

Слуга Мартинеса. Мой господин, дон Педро Мартинес, услышав про бальзам, просит отпустить ему одну порцию.

Паломек. Эге-ге!.. (*Слуге.*) Давай два реала.

Слуга Мартинеса. Пожалуйте. Только самого крепкого. (*Дает деньги Паломеку.*)

Мариторнес. Лучше никто бы не подогрел, сеньор!

Дон Кихот (*простирает руки над кастрюлей и начинает шептать какие-то заклинания. Паломек, Слуга Мартинеса и Погонщик мулов снимают шапки.*) Можно пить.

Паломек. Стой, стой, по порядку! (*Разливают бальзам по кружкам.*)

Слуга Мартинеса убегает во флигель. Остальные пьют бальзам. Первому делается плохо Дон Кихоту, он падает навзничь.

Ой!.. Ой!.. Ой!.. Что же это такое?!

Мариторнес. Хозяин, священника мне... Требую священника за мою верную службу... смерть пришла...

Музыка во флигеле внезапно прекращается, загремела посуда, послышался хохот.

Санчо. Будь он проклят, ваш бальзам, отныне... и во веки веков!..

Паломек срывается с места и убегает, за ним устремляются Мариторнес и Работник. Из флигеля выбегает Дон Педро Мартинес, а за ним — его Слуга с кружкой.

Мартинес. Исчадие ада! Чем же ты напоил меня?! Палач!..

Слуга Мартинеса. Два реала, сеньор, два реала я отдал, как одну полушку… Наилучший бальзам… вы же сами приказали!

Мартинес. Убийца! (*Убегает.*)

Слуга Мартинеса. С чего это он так взбесился? Надо попробовать. (*Допивает остатки бальзама, некоторое время топчется на месте, затем убегает вслед за Мартинесом.*)

Санчо. Что же это вы, сеньор, делаете с людьми?

Погонщик мулов (*медленно пьет бальзам, вытирает рот, обращается к Санчо*). Что, худо, приятель?

Санчо. Уйди от меня…

Погонщик мулов. Я тебе скажу, в чем дело: мало перцу положили, а так он правильный бальзам. Правда, он забористый бальзам, мы им мулов постоянно лечим. Ну, сперва мул бьется очень сильно, лягается, но зато потом целый год как железный и летит, как стрела из арбалета. Ты не бойся. Сейчас тебе станет еще хуже, а зато потом вскочишь здоровый.

Санчо. Уйди, проклятый, куда-нибудь в сторону! Мне нехорошо, когда ты торчишь перед глазами.

Погонщик мулов. Не унывай, друг! Эге! Кажется, и на меня действует. (*Уходит.*)

Дон Кихот. Я знаю, Санчо, отчего тебе стало худо: ты не посвящен в рыцари, а этот бальзам…

Санчо. Так какого же дьявола, сеньор, вы меня не предупредили!..

Дон Кихот. А мне легче стало. Теперь бы только заснуть... (*Засыпает.*)

Возвращаются Паломек, Мариторнес, Работник.

Паломек. Вот принесло чертей ко мне на постоялый двор! То есть никогда ничего подобного не было в жизни!

Мартинес (*появляется в сопровождении своего Слуги*). А знаешь, это хорошая штука! Сперва точно немного жутко становится, но зато потом облегчение! Купи еще кружку у этого коновала.

Слуга Мартинеса. Слушаю, сеньор. (*Уходит во флигель с Мартинесом.*)

В сарай возвращается Погонщик мулов.

Санчо. Ох... за что же такое наказание? Днем две взбучки подряд, а вечером этот бальзам... Что же, сударь, вы доконать меня хотите? Что это за жизнь, я вас спрашиваю?

Погонщик мулов. Какие взбучки? Ты же говорил, что со скалы упал?

Санчо. Не приставай ко мне...

Быстро темнеет, вырезывается луна. У Паломека в окне появляется свет, потом гаснет. Во флигеле некоторое время еще слышен хохот, пение, звон стаканов.

Мартинес (*во флигеле*). Ваше здоровье, сеньоры!

Потом и флигель затихает, окна гаснут. Во дворе появляется Мариторнес.

Мариторнес (*прокрадываясь к сараю*). Кажется, все заснули. (*Прислушивается.*) Да, спят... Ох, страшно!.. Эй, погонщик, ты спишь?

Дон Кихот (*просыпаясь*). Что слышу я?

Мариторнес в сарае ищет постель Погонщика.

(*Взяв Мариторнес за руку.*) Очаровательная сеньора!

Мариторнес. Это ты? Видишь, ты шепнул мне...

Дон Кихот. О страстная сеньора, как бы я хотел быть в должной мере признателен вам за ту честь...

Погонщик мулов (*просыпаясь*). Это что такое?

Мариторнес. Ах, не тот, не тот! Это не ты!

Дон Кихот. Судьба швырнула меня, израненного...

Мариторнес. Отпустите меня, сеньор!

Дон Кихот. Сеньора...

Погонщик мулов. Эге-ге! Да эта козлиная борода, оказывается, хват! А поглядеть на него — тихоня! Бальзам приготовляет, со скалы упал...

Дон Кихот. Я понимаю ваше намерение...

Мариторнес. Пустите меня, сеньор!

Дон Кихот. Знайте, сеньора, что я верен несравненной Дульсинее Тобосской...

Погонщик мулов. Ну, к черту это пение! (*Подкрадывается к Дон Кихоту, ударяет его тазом по голове.*)

Дон Кихот. Ах, коварный мавр!

Мариторнес. Ах!

Санчо (*проснувшись*). Кто тут? Кто тут? Ты что здесь делаешь, голубушка? (*Схватывает Мариторнес за руку.*)

Погонщик мулов. А ты не лезь не в свое дело! (*Ударяет Санчо.*)

Санчо. Ох, это опять, стало быть, начинается? (*Ныряет под попону.*)

Дон Кихот (*схватываясь за меч*). Ну погоди же, вероломный, напавший на меня из-за угла! Эй, Санчо!

Санчо. Я сплю, сударь.

Мариторнес. Куда же деваться-то мне?!

Погонщик мулов. Не сюда, не сюда! Хозяин проснулся, увидит тебя!

В окне у Паломека свет.

Лезь через крышу! (*Подсаживает Мариторнес, и та скрывается из сарая. Бросается на свою постель и укрывается попоной.*)

Дон Кихот. Замок очарован! Здесь волшебники! А! Вот вы где притаились, злостные создания! Вас много, я один, но вы не устрашите меня! (*Поражает мечом бурдюк с вином.*) Вот хлынула черная кровь! Ты повержен, злодей!

Мартинес (*во флигеле*). Что случилось? Эй, огня!

Эрнандес (*во флигеле*). Огня, огня!

Паломек (*выбегает во двор*). Что там случилось в сарае? Эй! Голову прозакладываю, что это штуки проклятой Мариторнес! Эй! Мариторнес, где ты, подлая?

Дон Кихот. Враг побежден!

Мариторнес (*в окне*). Чего вам? Чего вас ночью будит нечистая сила, хозяин?

Паломек. Как? Ты здесь? Я был уверен, что ты уже в сарае!

Во двор вбегают Эрнандес, Мартинес со шпагой, его Слуга с кочергой и еще один Постоялец со светильником.

Мартинес. Кто напал? Что случилось? Эй, кто убит?

Эрнандес. Воры? Где воры? Эй, там, в сарае!..

Светает.

Дон Кихот. Убит мой враг, почтенный кастелян! Смотрите, вот бежит его кровь!

Паломек (*уронив светильник*). Я желал бы видеть вашу кровь вместо этой! Смотрите, сеньоры, этот сумасшедший пропорол бурдюк с вином!

Погонщик мулов (*делая вид, что проснулся*). А, какого черта не дают спать?

Санчо. Да, в самом деле, что же это спать не дают ни мне, ни моему рыцарю?

Дон Кихот. Остальные бежали, Санчо! Скорее в путь, мы их догоним!

Санчо. Да, сеньор, нам пора, я предчувствую, что здесь будет большая кутерьма. (*Бежит к конюшне, выводит Росинанта и осла.*)

Появляются Работник и Мариторнес.

Паломек. Полюбуйтесь, сеньоры, на то, что натворила эта парочка полоумных! Вино, мое лучшее вино!

Эрнандес. Действительно, это какие-то черти! Не правда ли, сеньор Мартинес?

Мартинес. Это — который делал бальзам?

Слуга Мартинеса. Он самый, сударь.

Мартинес. Прекрасный бальзам, только почему их леший будит по ночам?[32]

Дон Кихот (*сидя в седле*). Сеньор кастелян, я в отчаянии, что мне приходится спешно покинуть ваш

[32] A леший is a creature from Russian folklore similar to a wood goblin. The powers attributed to it range from leading peasants astray and infecting them with diseases to abducting small children and young women and hiding woodcutters' axes. In colloquial Russian, леший can be used as a synonym for the devil. To a Russian ear the word evokes fairy tales and magic and creates a subtle link to Quixote's imagined existence in a fantastic world.

гостеприимный замок. Я должен отправиться в погоню за моими врагами. Благодарю вас за внимание, оказанное мне и моему оруженосцу, и желаю вам всего хорошего.

Погонщик мулов. Опять запел! Накостылять бы ему шею на прощанье!

Санчо. Не надо длинных речей, сеньор, едем.

Паломек. Оставьте ваши благодарности при себе, господин аптекарь, и платите за ночлег, за корм, а главное, за вино, которое вы погубили на моем постоялом дворе!

Дон Кихот. Как, это постоялый двор? Вы говорите правду? Значит, я был в заблуждении, полагая, что нахожусь в замке. Но, впрочем, это ничего не значит. Жар и зной, непогода и холод терзают странствующих рыцарей в то время, как они скитаются по свету для блага человечества, и никто и никогда, нигде не смел требовать с них какой-либо платы. Таков устав ордена. Прощайте.

Паломек. Стойте! Правосудие, сеньоры!

Дон Кихот (*угрожая копьем*). Прочь, если дорожишь жизнью, жадный трактирщик! (*Уезжает в ворота.*)

Паломек. Правосудие! Правосудие! Меня ограбили! Держите второго! (*Работнику.*) Закрывай ворота!

Санчо окружают.

Ты будешь платить, каналья, или нет?

Санчо. Жар и зной... терзают наш орден... Пропустите-ка меня.

Паломек. Вы видите, сеньоры, каковы мошенники?!

Эрнандес. Проучить его, негодяя?

Мартинес. Повторяю: бальзам великолепный, но он действительно жулик! Давай сюда одеяло!

Санчо. На помощь, сеньор!.. Не бегите, презренные созданья! На помощь!..

Голова Дон Кихота появляется за оградой. На Санчо набрасываются и валят его на одеяло.

Дон Кихот (*за оградой*). Гнусные негодяи! Отпустите сейчас же моего оруженосца!

Санчо подбрасывают.

Паломек (*в паузе*). Ты будешь платить?

Санчо. И рад бы, да не могу...

Паломек. Швыряйте его в самое небо!

Мартинес. Довольно! Ну его к черту!

Паломек (*овладевая бурдюком Санчо*). Отдавай бурдюк и убирайся с глаз моих, темный мошенник.

Все расходятся со двора, кроме Мариторнес и Погонщика мулов.

Погонщик мулов. А мне нравится этот парень! Упорный парень! Ведь так-таки и не заплатил. Молодец!

Мариторнес. На, попей воды.

Дон Кихот (*за оградой*). Не пей эту воду, Санчо, она отравлена. У меня осталась еще склянка бальзама, она тотчас поставит тебя на ноги.

Санчо. Поберегите, сеньор, ваш бальзам для Рейнальдоса Монтальбана, для золотого идола Магомета и для всех чертей! А меня оставьте в покое!

Дон Кихот. Несчастный! Я не могу видеть, как ты отравляешь себя! Опомнись! (*Отъезжает от ограды.*)

Санчо. Дай-ка мне, девушка, винца. (*Шепотом.*) Тебе я заплачу.

Мариторнес приносит вина.

Погонщик мулов. Давай и мне за компанию.

Санчо. Спасибо тебе. (*Дает монету Мариторнес.*)

Погонщик мулов. Не надо, я тебя угощаю. Ты мне понравился за свой твердый характер.

Санчо. Вы — единственные добрые созданья среди всех мучителей на этом постоялом дворе. Правда, девушка, твое поведение немного предосудительно, но я не люблю осуждать людей. Спасибо вам, прощайте.

Мариторнес. Прощай.

Погонщик мулов (*провожая Санчо к воротам*). Перцу надо больше класть, это ты запомни. Тогда смело продавайте по реалу кружка.

КАРТИНА ЧЕТВЕРТАЯ

У Дон Кихота. День. В комнате — Антония, Ключница, Перес и Николас

Перес. Итак, что же делать нам теперь? Мудрость недаром говорит, что подобное лечится подобным...

Николас. Я совершенно с вами согласен, почтеннейший мой кум.

Перес. Жажда подвигов выгнала бедного идальго из дому. Дадим же ему возможность совершить такой подвиг, который привел бы его домой. И вот что я придумал вместе с сеньором Николасом: вы, Антония, примете на себя роль очарованной принцессы.

Антония. Я не понимаю вас, сеньор лиценциат.

Николас. Стоит развязать этот узел — и вы сразу все поймете! (*Вынимает из узла богатый женский наряд, большую привязную бороду, гитару и маски.*)

Перес. Запомните, Антония, что вы — очарованная принцесса, дочь короля Тинакрио Мудрого и королевы Харамильи, наследница великого королевства Микомикон в Гвинее. Злой великан Пандофиландо Косой отнял у вас царство. Мы поедем вдогонку за вашим безумным дядюшкой, и вы обратитесь к нему со слезной просьбой заступиться за вас и отвоевать это царство у великана.[33]

Ключница. Господи, помилуй нас, грешных!

Николас. И не будь я цирюльник здешнего села, если он не последует за вами куда угодно!

Перес. Но внушите ему, что путь в ваше королевство лежит через Ламанчу.

Антония. Ах, теперь поняла!

Николас (*подает платье и маску Антонии*). Переодевайтесь, Антония.

Антония. Сейчас. (*Уходит в соседнюю комнату.*)

Ключница. Милосердное небо, на какие уловки приходится пускаться, чтобы возвратить к родному очагу нашего бедного хозяина! Пусть дьявол и разбойник Варрава унесут в преисподнюю рыцарские книги, погубившие самый светлый ум Ламанчи! А вместе с книгами и толстобрюхого Санчо, сманившего сеньора Алонсо из дому! (*Уходит.*)

Перес. Приступим, дорогой кум.

Перес надевает бороду. Николас одевается в женское платье и головной убор, надевает маску, берет гитару, Антония входит в богатом наряде, в маске.

---

[33] The scene parallels a story from volume 1 of the novel, in which the priest and barber recruit Dorotea, whom they encounter in the Sierra Morena Mountains, to enact a chivalric tale to lure Don Quixote back home. In the novel, Dorotea plays Princess Micomicona.

Антония. Вы ли это, маэсе Николас? Кто же вы такой теперь?

Николас. Я — дуэнья, сопровождающая вас в вашем скорбном изгнании. Запомните мое имя — Долорида. (*Наигрывает на гитаре.*)

Перес. Я же, сеньора Антония, ваш дядюшка, брат убитого короля Тинакрио.

Антония. Поняла, поняла!

Перес. Важно только одно — заманить его сюда, а там уж мы что-нибудь придумаем, глядя по обстоятельствам.

Во двор дома в это время въезжает на своем осле Санчо, и в тот же момент из кухни выбегает Ключница.

Ключница. Это он! Да, это он! Меня не обманывают мои бедные глаза!

Санчо. Это я, сеньора ключница.

Ключница. Да это он, смутьян и всесветный бродяга!

Санчо. Да, это она...

Антония, Перес и Николас бросаются к окну, смотрят на эту сцену.

Ключница. Отвечай, поганый попугай, повторяющий чужие слова, где сеньор Кихано? Куда ты девал его? Ты один? Отвечай, ты один вернулся?

Санчо. Я не настолько глуп, сеньора ключница, чтобы утверждать, что нас двое. Вы же видите, что я один.

Ключница. Куда же ты девал, окаянный, сеньора Алонсо?

Санчо. Кто-нибудь, у кого доброе сердце, на помощь! Дорогая ключница, меня били за эти дни много раз, но каждый раз били к концу нашего пребывания где-нибудь, а теперь трепка начинается, лишь только я сунул нос в ворота! Помогите!

Антония. О боже! Она терзает его!

Перес. Погодите, погодите, мы сейчас все узнаем.

Ключница. Куда ты девал моего господина?

Санчо. Спасите меня от адской ключницы! Сеньор цел, жив и здоров! Вы не имеете права бить меня! Не сегодня-завтра я стану губернатором!

Ключница. Слыхали вы что-нибудь подобное, добрые люди? Кто вбил тебе в голову эту мысль, алчный чурбан? Где сеньор Кихано? Почему ты молчишь?

Санчо. О боже праведный! И нет никого, кто вырвал бы меня из рук ключницы, терзающей меня, как ястреб куренка!

Перес. Сеньора ключница!.. Почтенная сеньора, подавите свой гнев, который вы обрушиваете на этого ни в чем не повинного человека!

Санчо. Это кто же такой?

Ключница. Пусть он скажет, где он покинул сеньора Алонсо!

Перес. Мы узнаем это скорее, чем вы. Я очень советую вам, сеньора ключница, продолжать готовить нам пищу, нам предстоит неблизкий путь.

Ключница. Ну хорошо, сеньор. Но узнайте, умоляю вас, где бедный мой господин! (*Уходит.*)

Перес. Почтеннейший, оставьте вашего осла и подите сюда.

Санчо (*входя в комнату*). Доброго здоровья, глубокоуважаемые сеньоры и сеньор!

Перес. Позвольте, да это он!

Николас. Верить ли мне моим глазам?

Перес. Да, принцесса, это он, Санчо Панса, оруженосец прославленного рыцаря Дон Кихота. Я не успокоюсь до тех пор, пока не облобызаю его!

Антония. Нет, нет, первая это сделаю я!

Николас. Нет, уж пустите меня первую! (*Обнимает Санчо.*) Моя душа взволнована, а в этих случаях единственно, что может успокоить меня, — это музыка. (*Играет на гитаре.*)

Перес и Антония обнимают Санчо.

Санчо. Покорнейше вас благодарю за музыку и ласки, которыми вы осыпали меня, но скажите, откуда вы меня знаете?

Перес. Слава вашего рыцаря уже побежала по свету, как огонь бежит по лесу, а следом за ней, конечно, побежала и ваша слава. Садитесь, любимый нами всеми оруженосец, и скажите нам, где же ваш рыцарь?

Санчо. Сяду я с удовольствием, так как очень устал после побоев ключницы, а где находится мой господин, я не скажу.

Перес. Но почему же?

Антония. Что слышу я? Жестокий оруженосец хочет отнять у меня последнюю надежду?

Николас. Почему вы не хотите открыть нам место, где находится ваш господин?

Санчо. Потому, что он приказал мне держать это в тайне.

Николас. Дорогой оруженосец, это странно! Вы уехали вдвоем, а вернулись один. Люди, чего доброго, могут подумать, что вы убили сеньора Дон Кихота.

Санчо. Пусть каждого, почтенная донья, убивает его судьба, я же не занимался этим никогда, и все знают это.

Антония. Нет, он скажет, где Дон Кихот. Знайте, Санчо, что перед вами принцесса Микомикон!

Санчо. Ага! Это очень интересно. Я никогда в жизни не видел принцессы.

Антония. Теперь, надеюсь, вы сообщите мне местопребывание вашего рыцаря, которого я разыскиваю для того, чтобы просить у него помощи и защиты.

Санчо. Нет, принцесса, не сообщу.

Антония. Так слушайте же, злой оруженосец, печальнейшую повесть моей жизни. Я жила в неописуемой роскоши в королевском дворце моего незабвенного отца Тинакрио Мудрого и безутешного ныне его брата...

Перес. Это я — перед вами.

Антония. Да, это он. Мне воздавали королевские почести, я сидела на золотом троне днем, а по ночам в парке принцы пели под моими окнами серенады.

Николас играет на гитаре.

Санчо. Повесть ваша очень интересна, принцесса, но только я не вижу в ней ничего печального.[34]

Антония. Слушайте, несчастный, дальше! В один ужасный день полчища великана Пандофиландо напали на наше королевство...

Санчо. А! Вот это хуже!.. Это я представляю себе ясно... Небольшое полчище погонщиков-янгуэсов напало однажды... и до сих пор у меня... впрочем,

[34] Sancho's choice of word for "story," повесть, is interesting. It derives from the Old Russian verb поведать and so suggests an Old Russian historical account (e.g. "Повесть о нашествии Батыяна Рязань," "Повесть о Калкской битве"). By this meaning, Sancho accepts the story he is told. But the modern meaning, "novella," implies that in this scene he knows the tale is a fiction.

не стоит об этом рассказывать. Ну и что же было дальше?

Антония. Мою мать, королеву Харамилью... и отца моего...

Санчо. Этого Тинакрио?

Антония. Да, да! Зарезали!

Санчо. Насмерть обоих?

Антония. Да, они в могиле оба.

Санчо (*Пересу*). А как же вы уцелели, королевский брат? Вы, наверно, сдались? В отчаянных положениях самый храбрый бережет себя для лучшего случая.

Николас (*Пересу*). До чего он придирчиво слушает, черт его возьми!

Перес (*Николасу*). Кажется, он немного растрогался.

Николас играет на гитаре.

Антония. И вот я в сопровождении моей дуэньи бросилась искать Дон Кихота Ламанчского, чтобы найти у него покровительство. Теперь-то уж вы мне, конечно, скажете, где Дон Кихот?

Санчо. Не скажу.

Николас (*швырнув гитару.*) А, чтоб тебя совсем!..

Перес. Милейшая дуэнья Долорида, вы напрасно сердитесь. Мне кажется, что оруженосец поступает правильно, сохраняя тайну, доверенную ему его господином. А скажите, добрейший Санчо Панса, что же вас-то привело сюда одного?

Санчо. Я привез письмо племяннице от моего господина.

Перес. Она уехала вместе с лиценциатом и местным цирюльником...

Санчо. Я его знаю, с Николасом.

Николас. Ну да, с Николасом. Прекрасный человек этот Николас!

Санчо. Хитрый очень.

Николас. Ну-ну-ну...

Перес. Погодите... в город, чтобы узнать что-нибудь о пропавшем дядюшке. А вы привезли важное письмо?

Санчо. Очень важное и, главное, приятное.

Перес. Скажите!..

Санчо. Оно заключает в себе приказание выдать мне в награду за верную службу двух ослят. (*Шарит в карманах.*) Ах!! Ах!.. Ах!..

Перес. Что такое?

Санчо. Ах я несчастный олух и дон болван![35] Ах я скотина и свинья! Будь я проклят! (*Бьет себя по лицу.*) Вот тебе! Вот тебе!

---

[35] The meaning of болван ("blockhead") derives from the Old Russian use of the word to refer to pagan idols made of stone or wood or

Антония. Что с вами, оруженосец?

Николас. Что с вами, дорогой упрямец?

Санчо. Бейте меня, сеньоры, прошу вас, потому что мне самому бить себя неудобно! Я потерял это письмо, а стало быть, потерял и ослят! Я ехал всю ночь, мечтая о том, как обрадуется им моя Хуана Тереса! Ах, ослятки мои, ослятки! Я дрожал от радости, я как будто уже ощущал вас в своих руках, я ласкал вашу нежную шерстку, я видел вас в моем хлеву! Кто мне поверит без этого письма, что мой господин действительно подарил мне этих ослят? Пандофиландо, зачем ты не зарезал меня вместо Тинакрио Мудрого?

Перес. Да, это плохо.

Николас. Да, придется вам расстаться с мечтой об ослятах! (*Играет на гитаре.*)

Санчо. Перестаньте играть! Что у вас за ужасная привычка! Как только случится что-нибудь гадкое, вы тотчас беретесь за гитару!

Перес. Успокойтесь, Санчо. Я знаю, кто может помочь в вашем горе. Это она, добросердечная принцесса Микомикон. Стоит ей сказать одно слово ключнице — и ослята будут в ваших руках.

Санчо. Сатанинская ключница послушается ее?

---

to the material itself. By combining the derogatory word with дон, Sancho indicates the enormity of his mistake.

Перес. Ручаюсь вам в этом. Но, само собой разумеется, что после этого великого одолжения вы скажете, где скрывается Дон Кихот.

Санчо (*подумав*). Скажу.

Антония. Ах добрый оруженосец! (*В окно.*) Сеньора ключница! Сеньора ключница!

Перес, Николас и Санчо высовываются в окно.

Ключница. Что вам угодно?

Антония. Вот что, дорогая ключница: потрудитесь выдать Санчо, по приказу сеньора Алонсо, двух ослят.

Ключница. Что? Что? Что вы сказали? Двух ослят?

Санчо. Ага!

Ключница. Да душу мою скорее вынут из меня, чем я этому негодяю...

Санчо. Ага! Что я говорил!

Перес (*тихо, в окно*). Если вы хотите увидеть сеньора Алонсо, вы немедленно...

Ключница. Этому... этому... ах, что вы сказали?.. Санчо? Ну, ему-то я охотно выдам двух ослят. Иди сюда, подл... иди сюда, Санчо, открывай хлев, бери ослят! О небо, что же это у нас происходит? (*Скрывается.*)

Санчо. О радость! О радость, и еще раз радость! Признаться, я вам не верил, а теперь убедился в том, что вы действительно принцесса Микомикон!

Перес. Да, но вы не забудьте сказать, где находится Дон Кихот.

Санчо. В ущелье, в Сиерра-Морене.

Антония. Что же он там делает?

Санчо. Он решил безумствовать в горах вследствие жестокости Дульсинеи Тобосской, подражая Роталанду и Амадису.[36] Я покажу вам туда дорогу.

Антония. Немедленно в путь, пока с ним не случилось какой-нибудь беды!

Санчо. Позвольте мне расцеловать вас, дражайший брат Тинакрио Мудрого! (*Заключает Переса в объятия, и у того слезает борода.*) Ах, что это?! Сеньор лиценциат?

Николас (*принимая в объятия Санчо*). Чего? Кого? Какой такой лиценциат? Где лиценциат?

Перес надевает бороду.

Санчо. У меня от радости помутилось в глазах и показалось, что вдруг Пандофиландо вам оторвал бороду и вместо вас появился лиценциат! Но теперь я вижу, что мне это померещилось!.. О радость!

[36] Amadís de Gaula was a Spanish knight-errant whose adventures were immortalized in print in four books by Garci Rodríguez de Montalvo in 1508. The story originates in the late post-Arthurian genre and was already in circulation in the fourteenth century. Roland and Amadís represent two different literary genres and two different ways of portraying a knight: the *Song of Roland* is an epic, *Amadís de Gaula* a novel of chivalry. In his desire for a literary creation of his own, Don Quixote must decide between them.

(*Выбегает во двор, бежит к хлеву, открывает двери его.*) Вот они, вот они, мои драгоценные! (*Кричит.*) Вот теперь, почтенная дуэнья, вы почему-то не играете на гитаре!

Николас играет на гитаре. Слышно, как подкатывает повозка.

Антония. В Сиерра-Морену!

Перес. В Сиерра-Морену!

Конец второго действия.

ДЕЙСТВИЕ ТРЕТЬЕ

КАРТИНА ПЯТАЯ

У Дон Кихота. День. К калитке подъезжает громадная колымага, на которой помещаются Дон Кихот и переодетые Антония, Перес и Николас. Николас, сидящий рядом с Возницей, играет на гитаре. Вслед за колымагой подъезжает на осле Санчо. Последним появляется Росинант, привязанный к седлу Санчо. Ключница выбегает из кухни.

Ключница. Здравствуйте, сеньор Алонсо! В час добрый! В час добрый! Как рады все любящие вас сердца, что вы наконец соблаговолили вернуться в родной дом! Ах, сеньор Алонсо! В час добрый.

Дон Кихот. Здравствуйте, добрейшая ключница!

Антония, Перес и Николас помогают прихрамывающему Дон Кихоту сойти с колымаги. Колымага отъезжает. Санчо с ослом и Росинантом пробирается к конюшне.

Светлейшая принцесса, позвольте представить вам нашу почтенную ключницу.

Антония. Мне это чрезвычайно приятно.

Дон Кихот (*знакомя*). Дуэнья... Ключница... Я уверен, что вы полюбите друг друга с первого взгляда.

Николас. Я мечтала об этой встрече! (*Обнимает Ключницу.*)

Дон Кихот. Прошу вас, дорогие гости, пожаловать в мой дом.

Антония, Перес и Николас, раскланиваясь, уходят в дом.

Где же Антония?

Ключница. Антония в доме, сударь, и уже принимает эту принцессу, не знаю, как ее зовут, и этого бородача.

Дон Кихот (*садясь на скамью*). Тсс... это не бородач, как вы выражаетесь, а высокопоставленный, хотя и глубоко несчастный, дядюшка этой принцессы. Я до сих пор под впечатлением трагедии его брата, гвинейского короля, зарезанного Пандофиландо Косым.

Ключница. Да бог с ним, достопочтенный сеньор! Ну зарезали этого гвинейца, что же поделаешь! Туда ему и дорога! Ведь вы его не воскресите?

Я же в вашу честь зарезала двух лучших жирных кур, чтобы варить вам бульон, и, право, от этого вы получите больше пользы, чем от гвинейского короля!

Антония (*в обычном своем наряде, выбегает из дома*). Бесценный дядюшка! Как я счастлива, что вы вернулись!

Дон Кихот. Здравствуй, Антония, ты позаботилась как следует о принцессе и ее дуэнье?

Антония. Как же, дядюшка! Вы слышите, дуэнья уже играет в моей комнате?

Санчо (*выходя из сарая*). Да, она играет, да не лишит создатель ее вечного спасения! Но если бы какой-нибудь очарованный мавр украл у нее гитару, я был бы счастлив! Ведь она играет по всякому поводу и во всякое время!

Дон Кихот. Твоя натура грубовата, Санчо. Музыку нельзя не любить. Где музыка, там нет злого.

Санчо. Даже жареные голуби могут надоесть, сеньор, если ими кормить человека с утра до вечера. А от этой музыки мне иногда хочется прыгнуть через забор. Позвольте, сеньор, мне отлучиться на короткое время, я хочу навестить мою Тересу.

Ключница. Ступай, ступай, Санчо, тебя никто не задерживает.

Дон Кихот. Ступай, мой друг, но возвращайся поскорее.

Ключница (*шепотом*). Ступай и не возвращайся больше сюда. Ты меня понял?

Санчо. Но мой господин...

Ключница (*шепотом*). Не возвращайся, если не хочешь лишиться и остатков бороды. Ты меня знаешь?

Санчо. Кто же вас не знает.. Вот в какие клещи я попал! (*Уходит.*)

Дон Кихот. Ну что же, Антония, пойдем в дом. (*Идет в сопровождении Антонии в дом.*)

Ключница уходит в кухню. В комнате Антония помогает Дон Кихоту снять доспехи, усаживает его в кресло. Из внутренней двери появляется Перес в своем обычном виде.

Перес. Здравствуйте, дорогой кум. Мы с маэсе Николасом узнали, что вы возвращаетесь, и немедленно явились, чтобы засвидетельствовать вам свое почтение.

Дон Кихот. Как я рад видеть вас, дорогой лиценциат. Антония, пригласи сюда королевского брата! Я хочу познакомить его с сеньором Перо Пересом.

Антония. Сейчас, дядюшка! (*Начинает целовать Дон Кихота.*)

В это время Перес ускользает во внутренние комнаты.

Я сейчас позову его, дядюшка. (*Уходит во внутренние комнаты.*)

Перес (*выглянув из дверей в бороде*). Сеньор Дон Кихот...

Дон Кихот. А, ваше высочество! Прошу вас, пожалуйте к нам сюда!

Перес (*в дверях*). Я не совсем одет, сеньор Дон Кихот.

Дон Кихот. Ничего, ничего, вы в дороге, никто вас не осудит.

Перес скрывается.

Сеньор лиценциат, познакомьтесь с королевским братом. Позвольте, а где же лиценциат? Ведь он только что был здесь! (*Идет к выходным дверям.*)

Перес без бороды выходит из внутренних дверей.

Перес. Я здесь, сеньор Дон Кихот.

Дон Кихот. Что за чудеса! А я вас потерял! Вы отлучились куда-нибудь?

Перес. И не думал.

Дон Кихот. Ээ... я все более убеждаюсь в том, что в доме моем нечисто! Антония, куда же ты ушла?

Антония (*в костюме принцессы и в маске*). Прошу извинить меня, доблестный рыцарь, что я задержалась...

Дон Кихот. Позвольте мне, очаровательная принцесса Микомикон, представить вам моего друга — сеньора Перо Переса.

Перес. Я счастлив, принцесса.

Антония. Я так много слышала о вас!

Николас (*в костюме дуэньи*). Вот и я, доблестный рыцарь!

Дон Кихот. А, наконец-то все собрались! Ах, нет, не хватает почтенного, но своенравного королевского брата.

Перес. Я сию минуту приведу его. (*Уходит во внутренние комнаты.*)

Дон Кихот. А где же маэсе Николас?

Перес (*в виде королевского брата*). Вот наконец и я.

Николас ускользает во внутренние комнаты.

Дон Кихот. Я хочу познакомить вас, господин королевский брат, с друзьями моими — лиценциатом и цирюльником. Маэсе Николас!

Николас выходит в своем обычном виде. Антония скрывается за пологом.

Перес. Так это он, добродетельный цирюльник, о котором вы мне так много говорили! Точно таким я представлял его себе!

Николас. А я, в свою очередь, горько плакал, слушая рассказы об ужасах, которые натворил Пандофиландо в королевстве вашего брата!

Дон Кихот. Антония, да иди же наконец сюда!

Антония. (*входя в своем обычном виде из-за полога*). Я здесь, дядюшка!

Перес скрывается за креслом Дон-Кихота.

Дон Кихот. Я хотел бы, чтобы ты выслушала из уст королевского брата о тех бедствиях, которые поразили королевскую семью. Сеньор лиценциат, пожалуйте поближе!

Перес (*выглянув из-за кресла без бороды*). Я слушаю внимательнейшим образом. (*Прячется за кресло, потом выглядывает в бороде.*) Да, этот отвратительный великан до сих пор стоит у меня перед глазами! (*Прячется за кресло, снимает бороду, становится перед Дон Кихотом.*) Что вы говорите, почтенный королевский брат!

Николас (*Антонии*). Мы пропали!

Антония (*Николасу*). Давайте скорее волшебника! (*Дон Кихоту.*) Да, да... Какой ужас, дядюшка!

Перес (*выходя из-за кресла в бороде*). Я лучше прекращу свой рассказ, любезнейшая сеньора племянница, если он вас волнует.

Антония. Ах, нет, нет, продолжайте!

Дон Кихот. Да, продолжайте, но я попросил бы всех сесть, а то должен сознаться, что у меня почему-то рябит в глазах...

Николас ускользает в соседнюю комнату. Перес бросается к окну.

... и по временам я даже не понимаю, кто передо мной.

За сценой раздается гром разбитой посуды. Перес опускает жалюзи, в комнате темнеет.

Что такое? Что здесь?

Николас (*за сценой*). На помощь! Здесь волшебник!

Перес. На помощь!

Дон Кихот (*схватывается за меч*). Где он?

Николас (*вбегая*). Волшебник похитил принцессу Микомикон на моих глазах!

Перес. А где же королевский брат?

Антония. Дуэньи тоже нет!

Дон Кихот. Этого следовало ожидать! Мы увлеклись беседой, и коварный прилетел неожиданно! Оруженосца мне! В погоню!

Перес. Бесполезно, бесполезно, сеньор Дон Кихот! Ведь не можете же вы лететь за ним по воздуху!

Николас. Я сам видел, как он, в черной мантии, пролетел над домом, волоча за бороду королевского брата!

Дон Кихот. Почему же вы не отрубили ему руку?

Николас. Промахнулся!

Дон Кихот. Ах, я не прощу себе этого! Где была стража? Щит и коня мне!

Антония. Дядюшка, молю вас, успокойтесь!

Дон Кихот. Принцесса была под защитой моего слова! Расступитесь! Вы поражены страхом, а я не боюсь его и догоню его, хотя бы он летел по воздуху с быстротой ветра! Пустите меня! (*Роняет меч, опускается в кресло.*)

Антония. Дядюшка, что с вами?!

Дон Кихот. Ах, открылись раны... Бессилие поразило меня вдруг... он очаровал меня...

Антония. Дядюшка, послушайтесь голоса любящей вас племянницы, вам нужно окрепнуть и отдохнуть. Драгоценный дядюшка, послушайтесь меня!

Перес. Послушайтесь нас, сеньор рыцарь, ложитесь в постель, благодетельный сон укрепит вас.

Дон Кихот. Да... я не в состоянии сейчас двинуться с места... колдовство сковало меня, как цепями...

Антония и Перес ведут Дон Кихота к постели и укладывают его.

Антония (*задергивая полог*). Он заснул. Бедный, бедный дядюшка!

Перес. Не надо отчаиваться, сеньора племянница. Сон освежит его, и, быть может, проснувшись, он станет спокойнее. Идемте отсюда, маэсе Николас. Прощайте, сеньора племянница, вечером мы придем его навестить.

Антония. До свидания, сеньоры, от всей души благодарю вас за все то, что вы сделали для дяди.

Перес. Мы лишь исполнили свой долг. (*Уходит с Николасом.*)

Антония уходит вниз, в кухню. Через некоторое время через калитку, ведущую с дороги, появляется Сансон Карраско.

Сансон. Вот он, милый моему сердцу двор! Два года я не был в родных местах, и ничего не изменилось здесь за время моего отсутствия... Вот и скамейка, на которой я сидел с Антонией два года тому назад... Кто дома? Отзовитесь!

Входят Ключница и Антония.

Антония. Ах!...

Ключница. Да неужто это он?

Сансон. Я, я, милейшая сеньора ключница!

Ключница. Праведный боже, кто бы мог подумать, что сын Бартоломео Карраско, простого крестьянина, станет ученым и важным господином! Ах, Сансон, до вас теперь рукой не достанешь!

Антония. Вы, пожалуй, не захотите теперь знаться с нами, Сансон, то есть я хотела сказать, сеньор Карраско?

Сансон. Многоуважаемая ключница, вы правы только в одном: я действительно стал ученым. Перед вами — бакалавр Саламанкского университета, у меня за пазухой четыре ученые степени, и я украшен лавровой ветвью![37] Но, ключница, я не стал важным, нет! И в доказательство позвольте мне обнять вас!

Ключница. Ах, Сансон, как радуется сердце, что вас не обуяла гордыня и вы по-прежнему ласковы с земляками!

Сансон. Антония! Как вы похорошели! Нет, нет, я чужд гордыни, будь я хоть двадцать раз бакалавр! (*Обнимает Антонию.*)

Антония. Сеньор бакалавр!

Ключница. Ах, в этом нет дурного, ведь он не чужой, он из нашей деревни. Вас вскормила одна и та же земля, одно и то же солнце грело вас!

[37] In Cervantes 2.3, Carrasco claims to have earned only four minor ecclesiastic orders and is therefore not qualified to be ordained as a cleric. There is no mention of a laurel wreath. Bulgakov misinterprets these orders as degrees and proposes that Carrasco is actually proud of the four.

Сансон. Нет, душа моя в волнении оттого, что я опять в родном селе, и в особенности оттого, что я вижу вас, Антония! (*Устремляется, чтобы обнять Антонию, но та ускользает, и Сансон обнимает Ключницу.*) И вас, почтенная Ключница! (*Протягивает руку Антонии, целует ей руку.*) Я не раз видел вас во сне.

Ключница. И я вас, дорогой Сансон!

Сансон. А у вас-то, Антония, есть ли хоть капелька радости оттого, что я приехал?

Антония. Я рада... рада...

Ключница. И я рада...

Неожиданно обе начинают плакать.

Сансон. Никогда не видел, чтобы радость выражалась в рыданиях. Что с вами?

Антония. Дядюшка помешался.

Сансон. Да что вы говорите?!

Ключница. Проклятые книги помрачили рассудок умнейшего и добрейшего сеньора!

Антония. Надел на себя заржавленные латы и убежал из дому, чтобы бороться с какими-то гигантами и спасать принцесс... Надел на голову цирюльный таз, размахивает мечом... Он совершенно замутил мозги нашему соседу Санчо Панса, назвав его своим оруженосцем, и тот убежал вместе с ним! Мы еле вернули его при помощи хитрости... Сансон, наверное, голоден, сеньора ключница, может быть, вы накормите нашего гостя?

Ключница. Как же не поесть, придя к родным и близким? Обед скоро будет готов. (*Уходит в кухню.*)

Сансон. Ваше горе меня глубоко тронуло, дорогая Антония!

Антония. Вы всегда были умным, а теперь еще стали и ученым. Если бы вы придумали, как нам избавиться от беды, я бы расцеловала вас, Сансон!

Сансон. Как вы говорите? Расцеловали бы? А знаете, у меня есть план! Целуйте меня, Антония!

Антония. Вы правду говорите?

Сансон. Я никогда не слыл лгуном в нашей деревне, Антония.

Антония. Я верю, что вы не обманываете меня, Сансон!

Антония целует Сансона, и в то же время голова Санчо показывается над забором.

Сансон. Ах, черт возьми! Да ведь это Санчо!

Антония. Он самый.

Сансон. Да, у меня зреет план. Оставьте меня с ним наедине, Антония.

Антония. Хорошо, хорошо, я верю в вас, Сансон! (*Оглядывается в дверях кухни.*) Сансон...

Сансон. Поцелуйте меня еще раз, Антония!

Голова Санчо опять появляется над забором.

Антония. Потом. (*Скрывается.*)

Сансон. А что же вы стесняетесь, почтеннейший? Входите, раз пришли.

Санчо. Аспид здесь?

Сансон. Про кого вы говорите?

Санчо. Про кого же это можно сказать? Про ключницу, конечно.

Сансон. Она в кухне.

Санчо вводит своего осла и ставит его в уголок.

Да это вы, уважаемый Санчо Панса?

Санчо. Если только это не штуки поганого волшебника Фристона, передо мной Сансон, земляк, сын старого Бартоломео?

Сансон. Да спасет нас небо от волшебников, это я!

Санчо. Черт побери, вы — бакалавр, Сансон! (*Целует его.*)

Сансон. Но скажите мне, дорогой сосед, куда же девалась половина вашей бороды?

Санчо. В доме повешенного не говорят о веревке, сеньор Карраско, или этого вы еще не проходили в вашем университете? Дай бог, чтобы у вас в кармане бренчало столько монет, сколько пучков волос надрали из моей бороды за последнюю неделю!

Сансон. Это грустно, сеньор Панса, но я надеюсь, что вы отрастите новую и она будет еще пышнее прежней.

Санчо. В свою очередь желаю, чтобы ваша ученость была так же пышна, как моя будущая борода.

Сансон. Э, как ловко вы отвечаете! Уж не учились ли и вы в Саламанке?

Санчо. Мне нет надобности учиться в Саламанке, и без этого я надеюсь получить губернаторство в самом скором времени.

Сансон. Как? Научите меня! Я тоже хочу стать губернатором.

Санчо. Сколько бы я ни учил вас, это вам не поможет. Для этого нужно стать оруженосцем великого рыцаря Дон Кихота Ламанчского!

Сансон. Да, сумасшествие заразительно, как я это теперь вижу.

Санчо. Что вы сказали?

Сансон. Я сказал это в сторону.

Санчо. Вы сказали это в мою сторону.

Дон Кихот (*просыпается*). Санчо! Ко мне!

Санчо. Слышите? Меня зовет мой господин.

Сансон. Очень хорошо. Ведите меня к нему, Санчо. (*Входит вместе с Санчо в дом.*)

Санчо. Сеньор, к вам гость.

Дон Кихот. Я очень рад.

Сансон. Позвольте мне, сеньор Дон Кихот Ламанчский, приветствовать вас! Слава ваша уже распространилась и достигла ушей покорного вашего слуги и скромного земляка — бакалавра Сансона Карраско.

Дон Кихот. Вы — сын Бартоломео Карраско?

Сансон. Точно так, сеньор, это я.

Дон Кихот. Я очень счастлив видеть у себя земляка, достигшего такой высокой ученой степени.

Сансон. Я еще более счастлив быть в гостях у рыцаря, слава о подвигах которого гремит по всей округе.

Дон Кихот. Садитесь, сеньор бакалавр. Вы навестили меня в момент ужасного несчастья...

Сансон. Вы огорчаете меня, сеньор.

Дон Кихот. Вечный враг мой; коварный волшебник Фристон — ученому нечего говорить, кто он, вы, конечно, сто раз читали о нем — только что похитил из моего дома находившихся под моим покровительством несчастную сироту принцессу Микомикон, ее очаровательнейшего королевской крови дядюшку и дуэнью Долориду!

Санчо (*в отчаянии*). Абиндараэс де Варгас!.. Будь я проклят со всей родней! (*Швыряет шапку.*)

Дон Кихот. Вы видите, сеньор бакалавр, даже эту, довольно черствую, признаюсь, натуру известие повергло в отчаяние!

Санчо. Как же мне не впасть в отчаяние, когда губернаторство ускользнуло из моих рук! А я уже держал в руках хвост губернаторской мантии, я мечтал о том, как вы разобьете войско великана и царство будет наше!

Дон Кихот. Так вот, сеньор бакалавр, что случилось!

Сансон. Я поражен всем этим! Что же вы теперь намерены предпринять?

Дон Кихот. Я немедленно пускаюсь за ним в погоню!

Сансон. И это ваше решение непреложно?

Дон Кихот. Вам ли это спрашивать, бакалавр? Для меня это долг чести!

Санчо. Ну, натурально, вы же не янгуэс какой-нибудь!

Сансон. Что?

Санчо. Ничего... была одна история, не стоит о ней рассказывать... пятнадцать человек лупят двух чем попало, выдирают половину бороды...

Сансон. О боже! (*Дон Кихоту.*) Но где же вы намерены искать эту принцессу и ее похитителя?

Дон Кихот. Какой-то добрый чародей послал мне сон, убеждающий меня в том, что злодей направился на северо-восток, во владения герцога. Туда же тронусь и я. Санчо, латы мне!

Санчо начинает надевать доспехи на Дон Кихота.

Сансон. Скажите мне, сеньор, что, если судьба будет неблагосклонна к вам и кто-нибудь из ваших противников победит вас?

Дон Кихот. Что же, если я буду повергнут в поединке, я приму условия моего противника точно так же, как он примет мои в случае моей победы.

Сансон. Немедленно поезжайте, рыцарь Дон Кихот!

Дон Кихот. Сеньор бакалавр, вы — человек, понимающий вопросы чести так же, как и я! Санчо, коня мне!

Выходят во двор. Из кухни выходят Ключница с блюдом и Антония.

Ключница. О горе! Сеньор Алонсо опять в латах! И этот толстый выродок уже выводит своего осла, чтобы ему переломили все четыре ноги!..

Санчо. Сеньора ключница... покорнейше прошу вас... (*Проворно въезжает в ворота.*)

Дон Кихот. Прощай, Антония! Прощайте, сеньора ключница!

Ключница. О горестная жизнь! Опять перед ним распахнулись ворота безумия и он бросается в них, чтобы погибнуть, закрыв глаза!

Антония. Что вы делаете, сеньор Алонсо, опомнитесь! Сансон, вы обещали мне, отговорите его!

Дон Кихот (*в седле*). Как, сеньор бакалавр, вы станете отговаривать меня совершить то, чего требует честь?

Сансон. Никогда в жизни! Поезжайте, рыцарь Дон Кихот Ламанчский, я горячо желаю вам удачи!

Дон Кихот. Прощайте же, мои верные дети! Я знаю, что вы любите меня, но не задерживайте меня больше и не горюйте обо мне! (*Уезжает.*)

Ключница. Какие слова найти мне, бакалавр, чтобы отплатить вам за то, как вы отнеслись к нашему горю! Вы своими руками толкаете несчастного безумца в калитку! Видно, ученость съела у вас последнюю совесть, и вы не только не посочувствовали бедным людям, попавшим в беду, но вы еще насмеялись над ними!

Сансон. Не спешите меня осуждать, не выслушав!

Ключница. Я не хочу вас слушать! Будь он проклят, ваш Саламанкский университет! (*Убегает в калитку вслед за Дон Кихотом.*) Сеньор Алонсо! Заклинаю вас всем святым, остановитесь!

Сансон. Антония!

Антония. Не подходите ко мне, Сансон! Я не верю ни глазам, ни ушам! Неужели вы хотели умышленно причинить нам зло? Скажите — за что? Что мы сделали вам, бедные?

Сансон. Антония!

Антония. Я знаю, вы из трусости, чтобы угодить сеньору Алонсо, вместо того чтобы его остановить, сами толкнули его на новое безрассудство! Вы обманули меня, Сансон!

Сансон. Да замолчите же! Я трус? Вы увидите, Антония, каков я трус, и горько раскаетесь в этих своих словах! Ведь я же сказал вам, неразумная девушка, что я хочу его спасти, и я его спасу!

Антония. Я не верю вам больше!

Сансон. Не впадайте в безумие, Антония, и не оскорбляйте меня! Я поеду за ним и верну его домой, но навсегда! Если же мне не удастся это сделать, то сам я не вернусь никогда! Это будет печально, Антония, потому что я летел сюда домой, чтобы увидеть вас! Ну что же! Значит, мне больше вас не видать! У меня нет времени разговаривать сейчас, я боюсь потерять его след. Прощайте, Антония! (*Убегает.*)

Антония. Сансон! Сансон! Я вам верю. Скажите мне, что вы задумали?

Сансон (*издалека*). Не скажу...

Ключница (*далеко*). Сеньор Алонсо, остановитесь!..

КАРТИНА ШЕСТАЯ

День. Зал во дворце Герцога.

Герцог (*входит*). Ко мне! Сюда!

Сбегается свита.

Сейчас в замке будет гость, тот самый сумасшедший идальго, именующий себя Дон Кихотом Ламанчским, со своим оруженосцем. Принять его со всеми почестями, и чтобы никто не смел подать и виду сомнений в том, что он странствующий рыцарь. (*Мажордому.*) А вас прошу и (*доктору Агуэро*) вас отправиться в загородный замок и приготовить все для приема оруженосца в качестве губернатора. Сказать ему, что он находится на острове Баратария.[38] Мы с герцогиней приедем туда через несколько дней посмотреть на его чудачества.

Мажордом. Слушаю, ваша светлость.

Доктор Агуэро и Мажордом с несколькими пажами уходят. Остается дуэнья Родригес, еще несколько дуэний и пажей. Звуки рогов. Появляется Герцогиня, отдает своего сокола Пажу. За Герцогиней входят Дон Кихот и Санчо.

Герцогиня. Милости просим, рыцарь Дон Кихот, в наш дом!

Дон Кихот (*у дверей*). После вас, ваша светлость!

Санчо входит первым.

---

[38] The name of the fictional island Sancho governs in Cervantes 2.45. It evokes the modern Spanish word for "cheap" (*barato*), which in Cervantes's time also meant "trick" or "hoax."

Великодушная герцогиня, простите этого неуча!

Герцогиня. Не беспокойтесь, сеньор, его простодушие и непосредственность очень милы.

Герцог. Я рад, сеньор Дон Кихот, вам будет оказан прием, приличествующий рыцарю.

Дон Кихот. Я счастлив, ваша светлость. (*Санчо.*) Если ты, вечный олух и шут гороховый, осрамишь еще раз меня, я отрублю тебе голову!

Санчо. Я сделал что-нибудь не так, сеньор? Обещаю впредь держать себя самым приличным образом, и если выйдет какая-нибудь промашка, то уж, во всяком случае, не я буду виноват.

Дон Кихот. Молчи!

Герцог. Прошу вас, рыцарь, в эту комнату — умыться с дороги.

Герцогиня уходит.

Санчо, помоги своему господину.

Санчо. После вас, ваша светлость. (*Обращается к дуэнье Родригес.*) Ваша милость, там у ворот остался мой ослик. Велите его отвести в конюшню, а еще лучше — сделайте это сами, я никому его не доверяю. Только имейте в виду, что он очень пуглив.

Родригес. Вы с ума сошли!

Санчо. Я? Нет. Мой господин рассказывал мне, что за рыцарем Лансаротом ухаживали сеньоры, а дуэньи — за его конем.[39] Правда, я приехал на осле, но, ей-богу, он стоит любого коня!

Родригес. Вот напасть! К нам в замок на осле приехал другой осел! Я, дуэнья Родригес, поведу осла в конюшню? Вот вам за это! (*Показывает Санчо фигу.*)

Санчо. Ах так? Очень хорошо. (*Дон Кихоту.*) Погодите, сеньор, не уходите. (*Тихо.*) Вот эта старушка сейчас мне фигу показала.

Дон Кихот. Ты лжешь, негодяй!

Санчо. Я сказал правду, сеньор. Как прикажете мне быть: оставить эту обиду без ответа?

Дон Кихот. Ты поклялся с меня голову снять, разбойник?

Герцог. Что такое, сеньор Дон Кихот?

Дон Кихот. Ах, ваша светлость, не слушайте его!

Санчо. Нет, как же не слушать? (*Герцогу.*) Фигу мне показала.

Герцог. Родригес? Да, у нее скверный характер. Ну что же, покажите такую же ей.

Санчо. Конечно, потому что мне обидно.

Дон Кихот. Ваша светлость!..

Герцог. Ничего, ничего, пойдемте умываться, сеньор Дон Кихот. (*Уходит с Дон Кихотом.*)

Санчо (*Родригес*). Вот вам от меня такая же.

---

[39] Lanzarote is the Spanish version of the name Lancelot.

Родригес. Ах!.. Ах!.. Ах!.. (*Убегает.*)

Санчо уходит вслед за Дон Кихотом. Музыка. Свита подает вино. Через несколько времени возвращаются Дон Кихот, Герцогиня, Герцог и садятся за стол. Санчо становится возле кресла Дон Кихота. Входит Духовник Герцога, садится поодаль.

Герцогиня. Скажите нам, Дон Кихот, давно ли вы имели известия от прелестной, очарованной Дульсинеи Тобосской?

Дон Кихот. Ах, светлейшая сеньора, мои несчастья бесконечны! Я победил уже не одного гиганта и всех их посылал к ней для коленопреклонения, но они не могут разыскать ее, так как злые волшебные силы превратили ее в простую безобразную крестьянку.

Герцог. Это печально.

Духовник. Что я слышу? (*Герцогу.*) Ваша светлость, а ведь вам придется за это дать ответ на Страшном суде. Вы, к общему соблазну, поощряете этих двух сумасшедших? (*Дон Кихоту.*) А вы? Как могли вы вбить себе в голову, что вы странствующий рыцарь, побеждающий гигантов и берущий их в плен? Перестаньте шататься по свету, глотая ветер и служа посмешищем добрых людей! Бросьте ваши безумства, вернитесь в свой дом, учите ваших детей, если они у вас есть, заботьтесь о хозяйстве!.. Где в Испании вы видели странствующий рыцарей, гигантов и очарованных принцесс? Где все эти нелепости, которыми вы смешите людей?

Герцог. Погодите, святой отец!..

Герцогиня. Святой отец, я умоляю вас!..

Дон Кихот. Нет, ваша светлость, разрешите ответить мне! (*Духовнику.*) Имейте в виду, что только то, что я нахожусь в гостях у герцога, да еще ваш сан сдерживают мою ярость, иначе вам пришлось бы плохо. Ну что же, я буду сражаться с вами вашим оружием — языком. Скажите мне, за какое именно из моих безумств вы осуждаете меня больше всего и приказываете мне учить детей, которых у меня никогда не было? Вы считаете, что человек, странствующий по свету не в поисках наслаждений, а в поисках терний, безумен и праздно тратит время? Люди выбирают разные пути. Один, спотыкаясь, карабкается по дороге тщеславия, другой ползет по тропе унизительной лести, иные пробираются по дороге лицемерия и обмана. Иду ли я по одной из этих дорог? Нет! Я иду по крутой дороге рыцарства и презираю земные блага, но не честь! За кого я мстил, вступая в бой с гигантами, которые вас так раздражили? Я заступался за слабых, обиженных сильными! Если я видел где-нибудь зло, я шел на смертельную схватку, чтобы побить чудовищ злобы и преступлений! Вы их не видите нигде? У вас плохое зрение, святой отец! Моя цель светла — всем сделать добро и никому не причинить зла. И за это я, по-вашему, заслуживаю порицания? Если бы меня сочли сумасшедшим рыцари, я был бы оскорблен до глубины души, но ваши слова я не ставлю ни в грош, они мне кажутся смешными!

Санчо. Прекрасно сказано, клянусь губернаторством, которое завоюет мне мой господин!

Духовник (*Санчо*). Опомнись, жалкий безумец! О каком губернаторстве мечтаешь ты, темный невежда?

Санчо (*тихо, Дон Кихоту*). Сеньор, он обругал меня!

Герцог. О нет, нет, тут уж вы ошибаетесь, святой отец! Тут же, при всех, я объявляю, что назначаю оруженосца Санчо Панса губернатором острова Баратария, входящего в мои владения.

Герцогиня. Я восхищена вашим поступком, герцог!

Санчо (*Духовнику*). Вот вам и темный невежда! Ах, как жаль, что нет ее здесь, моей жены Хуаны Тересы, она окоченела бы от радости.

Дон Кихот. Благодари, Санчо, светлейшего герцога за то, что наконец исполнились твои заветные мечтания!

Духовник. Ваша светлость, теперь я вижу, что вы проявляете такое же безрассудство, как и они сами! Но так как не в моей власти изменить ваши поступки, а порицать их бесплодно я не намерен, я ухожу! (*Уходит.*)

Герцогиня (*Дон Кихоту*). Вы хорошо ответили духовному отцу, сеньор! Все видят, что гнев его был безрассуден.

Герцог. Истинно так. Отправляйтесь же, Санчо, на остров, жители которого ждут вас, как майского дождя.

Дон Кихот. Разрешите мне, ваша светлость, дать ему несколько наставлений, чтобы в новом своем высоком положении он мог бы уберечься от ложных шагов.

Герцог. Это очень хорошая мысль, сеньор.

Герцогиня. Мы удаляемся и оставляем вас наедине.

Уходят все, кроме Дон Кихота и Санчо.

Дон Кихот. Слушай меня, Санчо, внимательно. Я взволнован, душа моя потрясена. Ты внезапно получил то, для получения чего иной тратит неимоверные усилия и, гонимый честолюбием или алчностью, прибегает ко всяким, порой нечистым средствам и, бывает, все же не добивается своего. Это я сказал тебе для того, чтобы счастье, свалившееся на тебя, ты не приписывал бы собственным заслугам, чтобы ты не надувался, как лягушка, и избежал бы насмешек над собой, а может быть, и злой клеветы, от которой не спасает никакое, даже самое высокое, положение. Гордись, Санчо, тем, что ты простой крестьянин, и не считай унизительным признаваться в этом кому бы то ни было. Нет надобности тебе доказывать, что бедный, но честный человек ценнее знатного грешника и негодяя. Не отрекайся ни от своего происхождения, ни от своих родных. Что еще мне хотелось сказать? Ах да! Ведь ты будешь судить людей! Это трудно, Санчо. Слушай же меня и не позабудь ничего. Когда будешь судить, не прибегай к произволу. Запомнил ты это?

Санчо. Запомнил, сеньор.

Дон Кихот. Ищи истину повсюду неутомимо, и пусть слезы бедного больше действуют на тебя, чем уверения богача, а в особенности его посулы. Руководись законом, но помни: если этот закон суров, не старайся придавить всей его тяжестью осужденного![40] Знай, что слава строгого судьи никак не громче славы судьи милостивого. Все может быть на суде.

[40] In the novel, chapters 2.42 and 2.43, Cervantes has Don Quixote discourse widely on the faith, morals, ethics, judgment, dress, appearance, hygiene, and behavior appropriate to a governor. For the play, Bulgakov concentrates on morals, ethics, and judgment.

Например, перед тобой может предстать твой враг. Что должен ты сделать в таком случае? Немедленно забыть обиду, нанесенную им тебе, и судить его так, как будто ты видишь его впервые в жизни. Бывают случаи, Санчо, когда судейский жезл вдруг задрожит в руке судьи, и, если это случится с тобой, не вздумай склонить его потому, что кто-то шепнул тебе что-нибудь и сунул звякнувший мешок к тебе в капюшон. Последнее в особенности запомни, Санчо, если ты не хочешь, чтобы я стал презирать тебя. И если ты когда-нибудь, в состоянии малодушия, вздумаешь склонить жезл судьи, то только из сострадания! Что еще мне сказать тсбе? Не будь грубым с низшими, Санчо, и — прошу тебя — перестань ты болтать! Знай, что болтовня может довести тебя до виселицы, и... будь опрятен. Если ты исполнишь эти мои советы, ты будешь счастлив в новом положении. Ты понял меня? Понял, ли ты меня?

Санчо. Не тревожьте больше свою душу, сеньор, я вас понял.

Дон Кихот. Погляди мне в глаза. Я верю тебе. Ну что же, давай попрощаемся. Мы больше с тобой не увидимся, дороги наши разошлись. Я отдохну здесь, в замке герцога, и тронусь в путь, туда, куда влечет меня мой долг.

Санчо. Эх, сударь...

Дон Кихот. Чего ты вздыхаешь?

Санчо. Я думаю о том, как это вы будете без оруженосца?

Дон Кихот. Я найду какого-нибудь другого.

Санчо. Пойдет ли еще кто-нибудь с вами, вот вопрос в чем! Знаете что, сеньор, я вам посоветую — вы тоже ему посулите остров. Я бы остался с вами, но...

Дон Кихот. Нет, нет, я хорошо понимаю.

Санчо. И позвольте мне, сеньор, на прощанье дать вам несколько наставлений. Что я хотел сказать вам? Да. Мое сердце чувствует, что вас будут бить, сеньор. Поэтому во время драки в особенности берегите голову, не подставляйте ее под удар. Она у вас полна очень умных мыслей, и жалко будет, если она разлетится, как глиняный горшок. Пусть уж палки гуляют по вашим бокам, одно-два ребра — куда ни шло!.. Что еще, сеньор? Да, там у вас осталась еще одна склянка этого Фьерабрасова бальзама. Вылейте вы ее, сеньор, к дьяволу, потому что если вас не прикончат в бою, то уж, наверно, прикончит этот бальзам. Исполните мои заветы, сударь, — будете счастливы в вашем новом положении! А я о вас буду очень скучать.

Дон Кихот. Спасибо тебе, что ты позаботился обо мне. Прощай и поезжай!

Послышались звуки труб, двери распахнулись, появляются Герцогиня, Герцог, пажи с губернаторским одеянием.

КАРТИНА СЕДЬМАЯ

Зал в загородном замке Герцога. Судейский трон. Кровать под балдахином. Слышны трубы. Санчо, в губернаторском наряде, входит в сопровождении свиты и садится.

Мажордом. Сеньор губернатор, на нашем острове Баратария издревле существует обычай, согласно которому новый губернатор, вступая в исполнение своих обязанностей, должен публично разрешить два или три головоломных дела для того, чтобы население узнало, умен ли новый губернатор или же он бесповоротный и окончательный идиот, и, в зависимости от этого, знало бы, что делать ему, то есть ликовать или сразу впадать в отчаяние.

Санчо. Давайте же сюда ваши дела!

Мажордом. Слушаю, ваша светлость!

Входят двое тяжущихся стариков, у Второго в руках палка.

Санчо. Что скажете, друзья мои?

Первый старик. Я, ваша честь, дал ему взаймы десять золотых и, когда настал срок, попросил его вернуть мне их. И тогда он ответил, что он отдал мне их. А на самом деле это неправда, а свидетелей у меня нет. И сколько я ни ходил по судам, я ничего не могу поделать, потому что он клятвенно утверждает, что эти деньги мне вернул. Заступитесь, сеньор губернатор!

Санчо (*Второму старику*). Он давал тебе десять золотых взаймы?

Второй старик. Давал, ваша милость, давал, но я их вернул ему.

Первый старик. Лжет он, ваша честь, никогда он мне их не возвращал!

Второй старик. Нет, он лжет, я вернул ему деньги сполна.

Санчо (*Второму старику.*) И ты готов присягнуть в этом?

Второй старик. Готов в любую минуту.

Санчо. Хорошо, присягай.

Второй старик (*Первому старику*). Будь добр, сосед, подержи мою палку.

Первый старик берет палку.

(*Взявшись за жезл Санчо.*) Клянусь в том, что я вернул ему десять золотых, которые он дал мне взаймы.

Первый старик. Как же небо его не покарает?

Второй старик протягивает руку, чтобы взять у Первого палку.

Санчо. Нет, друг, ты сказал правду, когда присягал, но палка-то пусть останется у него навсегда.

Первый старик. Но разве она стоит десять червонцев, ваша честь?

Санчо. Стоит! Стоит, или вместо мозгов у меня кирпичи! Взломать сейчас же эту палку!

Палку взламывают, и из нее выкатываются деньги.

Первый старик. Мои денежки! О мудрейший из всех губернаторов!

Второй старик (*падая на колени*). Простите меня, сеньор губернатор!

Санчо. Уходи, хитроумный мошенник! Но помни, что, если ты вздумаешь еще раз околпачить кого-нибудь, тебе придется худо!

Первый старик. О великий губернатор!

Мажордом
Свита } Великий губернатор!

Старики уходят. Появляется Женщина, а за ней — Свиновод.

Женщина. Правосудия! Правосудия! И если мне откажут в нем здесь, на земле, я буду искать его на небесах!

Санчо. А что случилось с тобой, голубка?

Женщина. Ваша милость, этот негодяй, встретив меня сегодня в поле, силой отнял у меня честь!

Санчо (*Свиноводу*). Ээ... да ты, как я вижу...

Свиновод (*в отчаянии*). Ваша светлость! Я, изволите ли видеть, свиновод...

Санчо. Ну так что же, что ты свиновод? Из этого ничего, дружочек, не следует... это... нет...

Свиновод. Я к тому говорю, ваша милость, что я действительно встретил ее сегодня в поле. Я, изволите ли видеть, продал сегодня четырех свиней... и... точно, случился грех... но с обоюдного согласия... и я даже заплатил ей.

Женщина. Лжет он!

Санчо. Ну, дорогой свиновод, есть ли у тебя при себе деньги?

Свиновод. Есть, ваша милость. Двадцать дукатов серебром.

Санчо. Ну что же, друг мой, плати.

Свиновод с отчаянием отдает кошелек Женщине.

Женщина. Да продлит господь жизнь нашего губернатора, защитника всех угнетенных! (*Уходит.*)

Санчо (*Свиноводу*). Чего горюешь, друг?

Свиновод. Душа моя тоскует при мысли о моих погибших денежках!

Санчо. Ну, если тоскует, то ты отними у нее кошелек.

Свиновод бросается вон. Послышался крик, потом вбегает Женщина, волоча за собой Свиновода.

Женщина. Сеньор губернатор! Этот разбойник среди бела дня при всех пытался отнять у меня кошелек, который вы мне присудили!

Санчо. Ну что же, отнял?

Женщина. Да я скорей расстанусь с душой моей, чем с этими деньгами! Он львиными когтями не вырвет их у меня!

Свиновод. Отказываюсь от денег!

Санчо (*Женщине*). Дай-ка сюда кошелек.

Женщина. Сеньор губернатор, как же так?

Санчо. Давай сейчас же кошелек сюда! Если бы ты с такой же силой защищала свою честь, как эти деньги, Геркулес не отнял бы ее у тебя. Уходи отсюда, жадная лгунья! (*Свиноводу.*) Нà тебе твой кошелек.

Свиновод. Благодарю вас, великодушный сеньор губернатор!

Санчо. Ну нечего, нечего, уходи отсюда и впредь не будь так легкомыслен.

Свиновод (*удаляясь.*) Да здравствует наш губернатор!

Мажордом. Население в восторге от вас, сеньор губернатор! Дела закончены, и ужин готов.

Санчо. Тогда и я в восторге, давай его сюда!

Появляется богато накрытый стол. Санчо усаживается за него. За креслом Санчо появляется доктор Агуэро. Лишь только Санчо прикасается к какому-нибудь блюду, Агуэро касается тарелки жезлом, и ее тотчас убирают.

Это что же значит?

Агуэро. Сеньор губернатор, я — доктор, назначенный специально для того, чтобы состоять при вашей особе и следить за тем, чтобы вы не съели что-нибудь, что может повредить вашему драгоценному здоровью. Это блюдо вредно вам.

Санчо. Так дайте кусок куропатки!

Агуэро. Ни-ни-ни! Гиппократ, отец медицины и учитель всех врачей, говорит, что...

Санчо. Хорошо, хорошо, если он говорит. Дайте мне кусок кролика!

Агуэро. Что вы, сеньор губернатор?

Санчо. Позвольте спросить, как вас зовут, господин доктор, и где вы учились?

Агуэро. Я — доктор Педро Ресио де Агуэро, уроженец местечка, находящегося между Каракуэлой и Альмадавар дель Кампо, а докторскую шапку я получил в Оссунском университете.

Санчо. Вот что, дорогой доктор Педро Ресио де Агуэро, уроженец местечка Альмадавар дель Кампо!

Вон отсюда ко всем чертям вместе с шапкой, полученной в Оссунском университете! Вон!

Агуэро. Сеньор губернатор!

Санчо. Вон!!

Агуэро убегает.

Подать мне кролика!

Мажордом. Слушаю, сеньор губернатор.

Санчо начинает есть. Слышен звук трубы.

(*Подает Санчо письмо.*) Письмо вашей светлости от герцога.

Санчо. Кто тут мой секретарь?

Мажордом. Я, ваша светлость.

Санчо. Читать умеете?

Мажордом. Помилуйте, ваша светлость!

Санчо. Читайте, хотя бы по складам, я разберу.

Мажордом (*читает*). "Дорогой губернатор, до меня дошли сведения, что в одну из ближайших ночей враг намерен напасть на вверенный вам остров. Примите соответствующие меры..."

Санчо. Отодвиньте от меня кролика. Пропал аппетит. (*Мажордому.*) Очень вам благодарен за прочитанное. Искренне сожалею, что вас выучили читать.

Мажордом. Тут есть еще кое-что.

Санчо. Добивайте меня сразу.

Мажордом (*читает*). “Кроме того, извещаю вас, дорогой губернатор, что враги покушаются на вашу жизнь. Будьте осторожны во время еды, вас могут отравить. Ваш герцог.”

Санчо. Я так и думал, что конец будет еще лучше начала. Убрать немедленно этот стол! Все убрать! (*Встает.*) Боже мой, боже мой! Дайте же мне хоть поспать спокойно, если уж мне не дают есть после всех трудов!

Мажордом. Слушаю, сеньор губернатор!

Темнеет. Санчо ведут к пологу, за которым он и скрывается; стол убирают. Зал пустеет. Слышна тихая музыка. Потом тревожный колокол, шум вдали.

Санчо (*выглянув из-за полога*). Это что же такое?

В отдалении выстрел.

Ну так и есть, сбылось написанное в этом проклятом письме! (*Скрывается за пологом.*)

Мажордом (*вбегая со шпагой*). Сеньор губернатор! Сеньор губернатор!

Санчо (*выглянув*). Что такое? Я надеюсь, что на острове все благополучно?

Мажордом. Никак нет! Враг внезапно напал на остров! К оружию, сеньор губернатор, к оружию! Становитесь во главе войска, иначе нас всех перережут, как цыплят!

Санчо. К оружию? Ах, если бы здесь был мой господин! Чума меня возьми! (*Скрывается за пологом.*)

Мажордом (*отдергивая полог*). Ваша светлость, что же вы медлите?

Свита (*врываясь с факелами*). К оружию!

Мажордом. Подать сюда большие щиты!

Санчо запаковывают в два огромных щита, так что он становится похож на громадную черепаху.

Вперед, сеньор губернатор, вперед!

Санчо. Какое там вперед, когда я не могу двинуться с места!

Мажордом. Поднять губернатора!

Санчо поднимают и выносят. Шум боя, блеск факелов. Щиты вкатываются обратно, и беспомощный Санчо остается лежать неподвижно, втянув голову в щиты. Вокруг него бешено топочет свита, за окнами крики и выстрелы.

Мажордом (*вскочив на верхний щит Санчо, командует*). Вперед, островитяне, вперед! Давайте сюда кипящее масло! Так, хорошо! Поливайте их! Сбрасывайте со штурмовых лестниц! Вперед! Вперед! Ага, они дрогнули! Перевяжите раненых! Сюда! Ко мне! (*Танцует на щите.*)

Свита.

Неприятель дрогнул!

— Он бежит?

— Победа!

— Победа!..

Бой затихает.

Мажордом (*соскочив со щита*). Победа! Развяжите губернатора!

Санчо развязывают и поднимают.

Поздравляю вас, ваша светлость! Под вашим предводительством армия островитян отразила неприятеля! Вы можете торжествовать!

Санчо. Дайте мне глоток вина.

Санчо подают вино.

Или, впрочем, не надо. Быть может, и вино у вас отравлено? Не надо. Приведите сюда моего осла.

Мажордом. Слушаю, сеньор губернатор.

Санчо. Расступитесь, сеньоры!

Свита расступается, и Санчо скрывается за пологом. К террасе, которая находится за залом, подводят осла.

(*Выходит из-за полога, одетый в свою обычную одежду.*) Ко мне, мой ослик! Ко мне, мой верный серый друг! (*Обнимает осла.*) Когда-то мы жили друг для друга:

ты для меня, я для тебя. И тогда у меня не было никакой заботы, кроме одной — напитать твое маленькое тело. И как счастливо текли тогда наши годы и дни и дома, и в скитаниях! А теперь, когда я из честолюбия поднялся на эту высоту, тысяча беспокойств, две тысячи печалей начали терзать мою душу и тело! Дорогу мне, сеньоры! Верните мне мою прежнюю жизнь! Я возвращаюсь к моему рыцарю, я нс рожден быть губернатором! Я умею подрезать виноградные лозы, а управлять островами не умею. Я привык держать в руках серп, и мне он нравится больше, чем губернаторский жезл. Я спокойнее сплю на траве, чем на тончайшей губернаторской простыне, и в моей куртке мне теплее, чем в губернаторской мантии. Прощайте же, сеньоры, прощайте! Но подтвердите перед герцогом, что я ушел отсюда таким же бедняком, как и явился к вам. Я ничего не потерял, но ничего и не присвоил. Смотрите, карманы мои пусты, я ничего здесь не украл! Прощайте! (*Садится на осла.*)

Мажордом. Сеньор губернатор, мы просим вас остаться с нами!

Свита. Останьтесь с нами!

Санчо. О нет, ни за что! Душа моя избита и изломана так же, как и мое тело.

Агуэро. Я дам вам, сеньор губернатор, наилучшие пластыри и лекарства!

Санчо. О нет! Никакими пластырями вам не вытянуть из меня моего упрямства! Я из рода Санчо, и если я сказал что-нибудь, значит, сказал твердо!

Мажордом. Мы полюбили вас, губернатор, за ваш ум и находчивость. Останьтесь с нами!

Санчо. Нет, нет, дорогу мне!

Мажордом. Ну что же поделать! Прощайте, Санчо Панса! Вы были самым честным и самым лучшим из всех губернаторов, управлявших этим островом! Прощайте!

Санчо. Прощайте! (*Уезжает.*)

Конец третьего действия.

ДЕЙСТВИЕ ЧЕТВЕРТОЕ

КАРТИНА ВОСЬМАЯ

Терраса и сад у Герцога. Огни в саду. Слышна музыка. Герцог и Герцогиня сидят на террасе.

Дон Кихот (*за сценой*). "О ревность, жестокая владычица в стране любви, обвей цепями руки!.."

Герцогиня. Опять им овладел припадок. Вы слышите, как он выкрикивает стихи под музыку? Мне жаль его. Я думаю, что, если бы не это злосчастное безумие, он был бы одним из умнейших людей. Когда его оставляют видения, он рассуждает здраво, мысли его светлы.

Герцог. Вы ошибаетесь, дорогая, он неизлечим, и остается желать только одного — чтобы его безумие хоть чем-нибудь развлекало людей.

Послышались звуки труб, входит Паж.

Паж. Ваша светлость, в замок приехал какой-то рыцарь и просит принять его.

Герцог. Какой рыцарь?

Паж. Его никто не знает, ваша светлость, он в латах и в забрале.

Герцог. А, плуты пажи! Конечно, это шутка мажордома!

Паж. Нет, ваша светлость, право, нет! Этот человек не известен никому, а назвать себя он отказывается.

Герцог. Ну хорошо, хорошо, во всяком случае, это забавно. Зови его сюда.

Паж уходит, послышались трубы, входит Сансон, в доспехах, с мечом и со щитом. На груди у него изображение луны.

Сансон. Простите меня, ваша светлость, за то, что я, непрошеный, явился к вам в замок.

Герцог. Я очень рад. Кто вы такой?

Сансон. Я — рыцарь Белой Луны.[41]

---

[41] In the novel, Carrasco is not viewed as a compassionate soul who intends to save Don Quixote from the Duke and Duchess. In Cervantes 2.12–14, he is an arrogant, college-educated neighbor who challenges Don Quixote to a fight as the Knight of the Mirrors but loses. He pursues Don Quixote throughout the novel, seeking revenge. In chapter 64, when he wins as the Knight of the White Moon, he obliges Don Quixote to return to his home. Cervantes paints Carrasco as the representative of reality who utilizes Don Quixote's belief in knighthood, disguising himself as a knight with a made-up story of his own version of Dulcinea, to vanquish him. The defeat of Don Quixote at the end of volume 2 propels him to his death.

Герцог. А, это очень интересно! (*Герцогине.*) Значит, в замке теперь двое сумасшедших. (*Сансону.*) Какая же причина вас привела сюда, рыцарь? Впрочем, какова бы она ни была, я рад вас видеть.

Сансон. Мне сообщили, что Дон Кихот гостит у вас. Я приехал для встречи с ним.

Герцог. Да, Дон Кихот здесь у меня, и я охотно дам возможность вам увидеться с ним. (*Пажу.*) Проси сюда Дон Кихота.

Паж. Слушаю. (*Уходит.*)

Герцогиня. У меня какая-то смутная тревога, герцог, нет ли чего опасного в этой встрече?

Герцог. Не беспокойтесь, дорогая, ручаюсь вам, что это шутка придворных.

Дон Кихот (*за сценой декламирует*). Да, смерть моя близка... Я умираю. И ни на что я больше не надеюсь как в жизни, так и в смерти!.. (*Входит в доспехах, но без шлема. Увидев Сансона.*) Кто это? (*Герцогу.*) А, ваша светлость! Отчего же вы не пригласите сюда

Bulgakov mentions only the last fight. He not only changes the plot, he also transforms Carrasco's character significantly. In the novel, Carrasco is motivated by his fascination with chivalry, while in the play he is motivated by his attraction to Don Quixote's niece. Furthermore, Bulgakov attributes positive qualities to Carrasco (that of creative artist) but then also has him leave Don Quixote in the Duke's power. In the novel, Don Quixote goes back to the Duke's palace precisely because he has been forced by Carrasco to go home and thus retraces his steps.

вашего духовника? Ведь он же говорил, что нет в Испании ни рыцарей, ни чудовищ! Он убедился бы теперь, что странствующие рыцари существуют! Вот, кроме меня, второй стоит перед вами! Вот стоит второй! Вы видите, огни плавают в его панцире и боевой отвагой горят его глаза — я вижу их в щели забрала! Итак, зачем же меня позвали сюда?

Сансон. Я приехал к вам, Дон Кихот Ламанчский.

Дон Кихот. Я здесь.

Сансон. Дон Кихот! Меня зовут рыцарем Белой Луны.

Дон Кихот. Что же привело вас ко мне?

Сансон. Я приехал, чтобы бросить вам вызов, Дон Кихот! Я заставлю вас признать, что моя дама, как бы она ни называлась, прекраснее вашей Дульсинеи Тобосской! И если вы не признаете этого, вам придется сражаться со мной. Один из нас будет повержен и примет повеления победителя. Я жду ответа.

Дон Кихот. Рыцарь Белой Луны, я, правда, ничего не читал и не слыхал о ваших подвигах, чтобы поражаться ими, но ваше высокомерие поражает меня. Нет сомнений в том, что вы никогда не видели Дульсинеи Тобосской, иначе вы бы не осмелились заговорить о ней так!

Сансон. Я смею говорить о ней, как я хочу, раз я вас вызываю! Отвечайте мне: принимаете вы мой вызов или нет?

Дон Кихот. Довольно, рыцарь Белой Луны, ваш вызов принят! (*Пажу.*) Подайте мне мой шлем и щит! Герцог, разделите между нами солнце![42]

Герцогиня. Будет поединок? Я боюсь!

Герцог. Что вы, герцогиня, это чрезвычайно интересно! Эй, факелов сюда!

Вносят факелы. Паж подает Дон Кихоту цирюльный таз и щит.

Где вы хотите стать, рыцарь Белой Луны?

Сансон. Там, где стою.

Герцог. Становитесь здесь, Дон Кихот.

Дон Кихот. Моя дама, помоги тому из нас, кто прав!

Герцог. Сходитесь.

Дон Кихот бросается на Сансона, успевает ударить его мечом. Левая рука Сансона повисает.[43]

---

[42] "Dividing the sun" was a way of positioning contestants in a joust so that one was no more bothered by the sun than the other.

[43] At twenty-three, Cervantes joined a Spanish contingent of the Papal Holy League and was on board the *Marquesa* for the Battle of Lepanto (1571) and the defeat of the Ottoman fleet. In the course of the battle he suffered a chest wound and an injury that left his left hand crippled for life. Not only does Bulgakov describe Don Quixote's and Carrasco's wounds, but he also ascribes one of Cervantes's wounds to both men. By so doing, he implies a certain identity between the author and the doubled characters.

Сансон. Ах!.. (*Устремляется на Дон Кихота, в ярости переламывает его меч, разбивает его щит и панцирь, сбивает с головы цирюльный таз.*)

Дон Кихот падает.

Герцогиня. Довольно! Довольно! Он повержен!

Герцог. Остановитесь!

Сансон. Нет, отойдите все! У нас с ним свои счеты! (*Приставляет острие меча к горлу Дон Кихота.*) Сдавайтесь, рыцарь Печального Образа, вы побеждены! Исполняйте условия поединка и повторяйте за мной: да, ваша дама, рыцарь Белой Луны, прекраснее Дульсинеи. Повторяйте!

Дон Кихот. Да, ваша дама... Нет, не могу! Я побежден, я побежден, я признаю это... но не могу признать, что есть на свете что-нибудь прекраснее Дульсинеи! Нет никого прекраснее ее! Но вот что вдруг стало страшить меня гораздо больше, чем острие вашего меча! Ваши глаза!.. Ваш взор холоден и жесток, и мне вдруг стало казаться, что Дульсинеи вовсе нет на свете! Да, ее нет!.. Мой лоб покрывается холодным потом при этой мысли!.. Ее нет!.. Но все равно, я не произнесу тех слов, которые вы хотите у меня вырвать. Прекраснее ее нет! Впрочем, вашему железному сердцу этого не понять. Колите меня, я не боюсь смерти.

Сансон. Я убью вас!

Герцог. Остановитесь, я приказываю!

Санчо (*появляется*). Сеньор Дон Кихот!.. Мой дорогой сеньор... Я вовремя поспел... я бежал с острова, я более не губернатор! Послушайтесь же совета своего оруженосца — признайте себя побежденным! (*Герцогу.*) Ваша светлость, не дайте отнять жизнь у честнейшего и мудрейшего идальго!

Герцогиня. Остановите поединок! Я не позволяю.

Сансон. Еще раз повторяю — оставьте нас! (*Дон Кихоту.*) Я освобождаю вас от этих слов. Живите со своим мечтанием о Дульсинее, ее на свете нет, и я удовлетворен: моя дама живет на свете, и уже потому она прекраснее вашей! Повторяйте за мной другое: я готов по требованию победившего меня рыцаря Белой Луны удалиться навсегда в свое поместье в Ламанче, подвигов более не совершать и никуда не выезжать!

Дон Кихот. Каменное сердце...

Сансон. Клянитесь, моему терпению приходит конец!

Герцогиня. Клянитесь!

Санчо. Клянитесь!

Дон Кихот. Я клянусь... я побежден...

Сансон вкладывает меч в ножны, отходит.

Кто же со мной?.. Санчо... Санчо, помоги мне, у меня разбита ключица.

Санчо. Помогите поднять его!

Пажи бросаются к Дон Кихоту, поднимают его.

Герцогиня. Послать за доктором!

Дон Кихота уносят, и на сцене остаются Герцог и Сансон.

Герцог. Шутка зашла слишком далеко, и теперь я требую, чтобы вы подняли забрало и назвали свое имя.

Сансон (*поднимая забрало*). Я — бакалавр Сансон Карраско из Ламанчи, рыцарем я никогда не был и быть им не желаю. Мне жаль было бедного идальго Алонсо Кихано, я его уважаю и люблю, и я решил положить конец его безумствам и страданиям.

Герцог. Гм... Ваш поступок благороден, бакалавр, я вижу, вы поплатились рукой за него. Ну что же, это делает вам честь! Но все же не могу не пожалеть о том, что похождения Кихано прекратились. Они были забавны, и он и его оруженосец развлекали людей.

Сансон. Не будем жалеть об этом, ваша светлость. Разве мало иных развлечений на свете! Соколиная охота, танцы при свете факелов, пиры и поединки... У знатных людей нет во всем этом недостатка, и нужно ли для развлечения рядить в шуты, увеличивая число шутов природных, человека, который этого совершенно не заслуживает?

Герцог. В ваших словах, почтенный бакалавр, мне чудится дыхание какого-то нравоучения, а к ним я вовсе не привык.

Сансон. Да сохранит меня небо от этого, герцог! Я не настолько дерзок, чтобы осмелиться вас учить. Считайте, что я рассуждаю сам с собой.

Герцог. Так знайте же, бакалавр, что для таких рассуждений наиболее удобным местом является ваш собственный дом. Если бы я знал о вашем замысле, я бы не допустил вас в замок!

Сансон. О, я догадался об этом и поэтому проник в замок в виде развлечения, желая этим угодить вашей светлости.

Герцог. Довольно! Прощайте.

Сансон поворачивается и уходит.

Эй! Выпустите из замка рыцаря Белой Луны!

Трубы.

КАРТИНА ДЕВЯТАЯ

Двор дома Дон Кихота. Закат. И комнаты и двор пусты. На холме, на дороге, за калиткой появляются сгорбленный и опирающийся на палку Дон Кихот с перевязанной рукой и Санчо, ведущий Росинанта и осла. На Росинанта нагружены доспехи, так что кажется, что верхом на лошади едет пустой внутри рыцарь со сломанным копьем.

Санчо. Вот она, наша деревня, сеньор! О желанная родина! Взгляни на своего сына Санчо Панса, открой ему свои объятия. Он возвращается к тебе незнатным, но чрезвычайно обогащенным опытом, полученным благодаря бедствиям, волнениям и несчастиям всякого рода. Он испытал все, начиная от града палочных ударов, сыпавшихся на его бедное, беззащитное тело, насмешек и издевательств людей, не понимающих, что такое оруженосец, и вплоть до неслыханных почестей, свалившихся ему на голову, когда он стал губернатором! И вот разлетелось это губернаторство как дым, прошла боль от палочных ударов, и сын своей родины явился туда, откуда он вышел, — под сень этих деревьев, к родному колодцу! (*Привязывает Росинанта и осла.*)

Дон Кихот в это время стоит неподвижно на холме, над двором и смотрит вдаль.

Племянница! Сеньора ключница! Я безбоязненно оглашаю воздух криками, потому что знаю, что вы, сеньора ключница, теперь уже не вцепитесь в меня своими острыми когтями и не осыплете меня бранью, от которой холодеет сердце у самого храброго. Мы возвратились навсегда!.. Сегодня суббота, она в церкви... Сеньор Дон Кихот, что же вы не входите к себе? Куда вы смотрите, сеньор?

Дон Кихот. На солнце. Вот он, небесный глаз, вечный факел вселенной, создатель музыки и врач людей! Но день клонится к ночи, и нсудержимая сила тянет его вниз. Пройдет немного времени, и оно уйдет под землю. Тогда настанет мрак. Но этот мрак недолог, Санчо! Через несколько часов из-за края земли брызнет свет и опять поднимется на небо колесница, на которую не может глядеть человек. И вот я думал, Санчо, о том, что, когда та колесница, на которой ехал я, начнет уходить под землю, она уже более не поднимется. Когда кончится мой день — второго дня, Санчо, не будет. Тоска охватила меня при этой мысли, потому что я чувствую, что единственный день мой кончается.

Санчо. Сеньор, не пугайте меня! У вас открылись раны. Всем известно, что когда начинает ныть тело, ноет и душа. Вы больны, сударь, и вам нужно как можно скорее лечь в постель.

Дон Кихот входит во двор, садится на скамью.

Идемте, сударь, я уложу вас, вас накормят, а сон принесет вам исцеление.

Дон Кихот. Нет! Я хочу поглядеть на деревья... Смотри, листва пожелтела... Да, день кончается, Санчо, это ясно. Мне страшно оттого, что я встречаю мой закат совсем пустой, и эту пустоту заполнить нечем.

Санчо. Какую пустоту, сеньор? Я ничего не понимаю в этих печальных и мудреных мыслях, несмотря на то что я необыкновенно отточил свой ум в то время, когда был губернатором. Неужели этот проклятый рыцарь Белой Луны — чтоб его раскололи в первом же бою, как перезревшую дыню! — своим мечом попортил не только ваше грешное тело, но и бессмертную душу?

Дон Кихот. Ах, Санчо, Санчо! Повреждения, которые нанесла мне его сталь, незначительны. Также и душу мою своими ударами он не изуродовал. Я боюсь, не вылечил ли он мою душу, а вылечив, вынул ее, но другой не вложил... Он лишил меня самого драгоценного дара, которым награжден человек, — он лишил меня свободы! На свете много зла, Санчо, но хуже плена нету зла! Он сковал меня, Санчо!.. Смотри, солнце срезано наполовину, земля поднимается все выше и выше и пожирает его. На пленного надвигается земля! Она поглотит меня, Санчо!

Санчо. Ах, сударь, чем больше вы говорите, тем меньше я что-либо понимаю. Я вижу только одно

— что вы тоскуете, и не знаю, чем вам помочь! Чем мне развеселить вас? Где прежний рыцарь? Ну хорошо, он победил вас, и больше вам не странствовать и меч не обнажать. Но вспомните, сударь, вы же хотели на крайний случай стать пастухом! И я охотно пойду с вами, сударь, если вы мне подарите еще парочку ослят, потому что я к вам очень привык... Да не молчите же, сударь! Ах, вот сама судьба приходит ко мне на помощь! А вот теперь я посмотрю, как загорятся сейчас огнем ваши глаза. Сударь, встаньте, идет ваше мечтание, к вам приближается Дульсинея Тобосская!

Из калитки, которая ведет в деревню, выходит Альдонса Лоренсо с корзиной. Увидев Дон Кихота, пугается.

Альдонса. Ах ты, горе какое! Вот он опять, сумасшедший идальго, на моем пути!

Санчо. Принцесса красоты, и королева величия! Перед вами покоренный рыцарь Дон Кихот Ламанчский!

Альдонса. И ты уже сошел с ума, толстый Санчо Панса? Или ты хочешь подшутить надо мной? Если так, то прибереги свои шутки для кого-нибудь другого, а мне дай дорогу! И не смей меня называть Дульсинеей! Я Альдонсой была и Альдонсой останусь. И так надо мной все смеются по вине твоего господина, несчастного дона Алонсо! Отдай эту корзину ключнице, а меня выпусти!

Санчо. Не слушайте ее, сеньор, она все еще очарована!

Дон Кихот. Альдонса!

Альдонса. Что вам угодно, сударь?

Дон Кихот. Вы боитесь меня?

Альдонса. Да, боюсь. Вы, сударь, так странно говорите и никого не узнаете...

Дон Кихот. Я вам скажу, кто вы такая. Вы — Альдонса Лоренсо, крестьянка из соседней деревни. Вы никогда не были Дульсинеей Тобосской, это я вас так прозвал, но в помрачении ума, за что прошу простить меня. Ну, теперь вы не боитесь меня?

Альдонса. Нет, не боюсь. Неужто вы узнали меня?

Дон Кихот. Узнал, Альдонса... Идите спокойно своей дорогой, мы вас не обидим. Санчо, не держи ее.

Альдонса убегает.

Санчо. Ну, сударь, теперь я вижу, что Белая Луна действительно все перевернула в голове у вас! Пусть меня повесят, если и мне не мерещится все время этот рыцарь... и, когда мы подходили с вами к деревне, мне все казалось, что он крадется за нами по полям.

Дон Кихот. Тебе не померещилось, Санчо, это так и было. Он действительно шел по полям за нами, хоть он и не рыцарь и никогда им не был. Да, он не рыцарь, и тем не менее он наилучший рыцарь из всех, которых мы с тобой встретили во время наших скитаний. Но он жестокий рыцарь.

Санчо. Клянусь детьми, этой загадки не поймет даже лучший губернатор!

Дон Кихот. Идем домой.

Идут в дом, причем Санчо несет доспехи. В комнате Санчо ставит их в угол, отдергивает полог.

Санчо. Ох, вот теперь я вижу, что вы больны, сударь! Ложитесь немедленно, а я сейчас слетаю за сеньором лиценциатом и цирюльником, они помогут вам. Я сейчас же вернусь, сударь! (*Убегает во двор и уходит, уводя осла.*)

Через некоторое время показывается Антония, входит во двор, а на холме за оградой, на дороге, возникает фигура Сансона в доспехах. Сансон идет медленно, и рука его, так же как и у Дон Кихота, на перевязи.

Антония. Помилуй нас господи! Кто же это там? Дядюшка? Нет, это не он! Уж не лишилась ли я от горя и сама рассудка? Я вижу рыцаря на закате, или это заходящее солнце играет со мной? Луна горит на груди у него, и перья колышутся на шлеме! Или мы все сумасшедшие, а дядюшка один здравомыслящий? Неужели он был прав, когда утверждал, что странствующие рыцари существуют?.. Кто вы такой?

Сансон (*входя*). Антония, это я. (*Снимает шлем.*)

Антония. Сансон!

Сансон. Осторожнее, Антония, рука моя болит.

Антония. Вы ранены, Сансон? Что с вами?

Сансон. Нет, нет. (*Освобождается от доспехов.*) В преисподнюю щит с изображением луны и туда же меч!

Антония. Сансон, вы говорили, что вы вернетесь только в том случае... Где дядюшка? Он не погиб?

Сансон (*указывая на дом*). Он дома. Я сдержал свое слово, Антония, и Алонсо Кихано никогда больше не покинет родной очаг.

Антония. Дома?.. Дома?! Если это так, Сансон, вы настоящий колдун! Недаром вас сделали бакалавром! Как же не сделать бакалавром самого умного человека на свете! Ах, что я говорю!.. У меня путаются мысли... Но это от радости, Сансон! Как же вы сделали это? Сансон! Сансон! (*Целует Сансона.*)

Сансон. Зачем же вы целуете труса и обманщика?

Антония. Не говорите так, Сансон! Какой вы злой, зачем вы мстите мне? Ведь я была тогда в горе, оттого и вырвались у меня эти слова. Нет, нет, Сансон, вы лучший друг наш, вы самый замечательный и благородный человек! (*Целует Сансона и убегает в дом.*)

Солнца уже нет, темнеет.

Дядюшка! Где вы?

Дон Кихот (*за пологом*). Кто тут?

Антония. Это я, сеньор Алонсо, я, Антония! (*Отдергивает полог.*)

Дон Кихот. Мне что-то душно, Антония...

Антония. Ложитесь! Ложитесь скорей опять!

Дон Кихот. Нет, нет, мне душно... и беспокойно... я лучше сяду здесь... и позови кого-нибудь, Антония, позови!..

Антония. Дядюшка, здесь бакалавр Сансон, позвать его?

Дон Кихот. Ах, он явился? Я ждал этого. Зови его сюда, но зови скорее.

Антония. Сансон! Сансон!

Сансон. Я здесь, сеньор Дон Кихот.

Дон Кихот. Зачем вы так называете меня? Ведь вы же прекрасно понимаете, что я не Дон Кихот Ламанчский, а тот самый Алонсо Кихано, прозванный Добрым, так же как и вы — бакалавр Сансон Карраско, а не рыцарь Белой Луны.

Сансон. Вы все знаете?

Дон Кихот. Да, знаю. Я узнал ваши глаза в забрале и голос, безжалостно требовавший повиновения... тогда, на поединке. Мой разум освободился от мрачных теней. Это случилось со мной тогда, Сансон, когда вы стояли надо мной в кровавом свете факелов в замке... Словом, теперь я вижу вас, я вижу все.

Сансон. Простите меня, сеньор Кихано, что я напал на вас!

Дон Кихот. Нет, нет, я вам признателен. Вы своими ударами вывели меня из плена сумасшествия. Но я жалею, что эта признательность не может быть продолжительной. Антония, солнце село?.. Вот она!..

Антония. Сеньор Алонсо, успокойтесь! Здесь никого нет!

Дон Кихот. Нет, нет, не утешай меня, Антония, дочка моя, я не боюсь. Я ее предчувствовал и ждал сегодня с утра. И вот она пришла за мной.[44] Я ей рад. Когда Сансон вспугнул вереницу ненавистных мне фигур, которые мучили меня в помрачении разума, я испугался, что останусь в пустоте. Но вот она

---

[44] The "she" Don Quixote speaks of is Смерть. The use of the personal pronoun here echoes Lev Tolstoy's similar anthropomorphizing of death in the description of Prince Andrei Bolkonsky's end in Война и мир, which Bulgakov alludes to here and in Белая гвардия as well.

пришла, и заполняет мои пустые латы, и обвивает меня в сумерках...[45]

Сансон. Вина ему, Антония, вина!..

Дон Кихот. Антония... Ты выйди замуж за того, кто не увлекался рыцарскими книгами, но у кого рыцарская душа... Сансон, у вас есть дама, и эта дама действительно прекраснее Дульсинеи... Она жива, ваша дама... Ключницу позовите... Нет, нет, Санчо!.. Санчо мне! Санчо!.. (*Падает.*)

Через двор пробегает Санчо, появляется в доме.

Санчо. Сеньор бакалавр! Помогите ему!

Сансон. Антония, вина ему! Санчо, огня!

Антония убегает.

Санчо. Сеньор Кихано! Не умирайте! Сеньор Дон Кихот, вы слышите мой голос? Взгляните на

[45] By allowing Don Quixote to welcome the darkness of death, Bulgakov sets his character free. Cervantes's Don Quixote puts his affairs in order in preparation for his end, but he never reflects on death philosophically. With its focus on the forgiving and liberating powers of the eternal night, the scene echoes the last sentences of the last chapter of Мастер и Маргарита: "Кто-то отпускал на свободу мастера, как сам он только что отпустил им созданного героя. Этот герой ушел в бездну, ушел безвозвратно, прощенный в ночь на воскресенье сын короля-звездочета, жестокий пятый прокуратор иудеи, всадник Понтий Пилат."

меня! Это я, Санчо!.. Мы станем пастухами, я согласен идти с вами!.. Почему вы не отвечаете мне?..

Антония (*вбегает со светильником*). Что делать, Сансон? Что делать?

Санчо. Он не отвечает мне!

Сансон. Я сделать больше ничего не могу. Он мертв.

Конец

Москва, 18 декабря 1938.

Work Cited in the Notes

Bulgakov, Mikhail. Мастер и Маргарита. Biblioteka Vekhi, 2001. Web. 6 Jan. 2014 <http://vehi.net/mbulgakov/master/>.